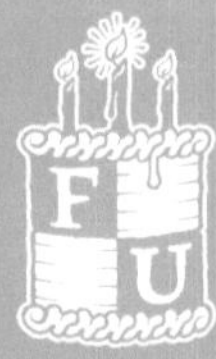

The
FROSTING UNIVERSITY KITCHEN WORKBOOK

An Absurd But Serious Cookbook

by Josiah Frosting

FIRST EDITION

PUBLISHED INDEPENDENTLY BY

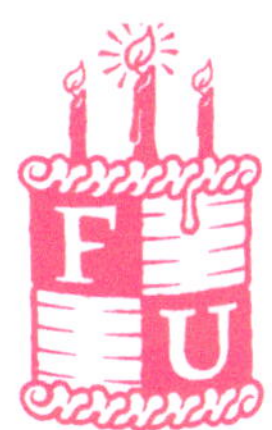

FROSTING UNIVERSITY PRESS

PORTLAND, OR

"Dulcis et Amarus"

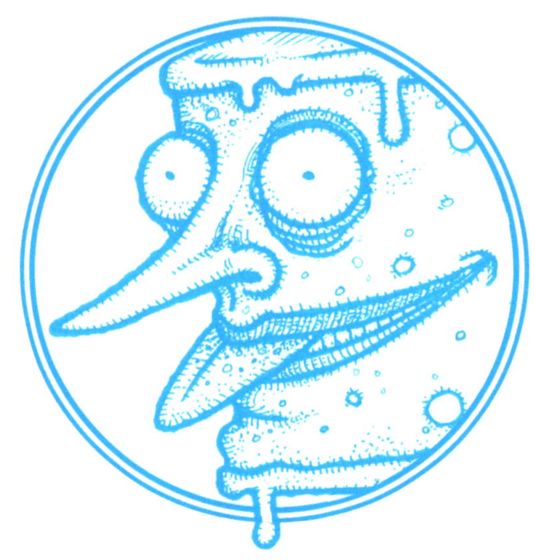

THE AUTHOR

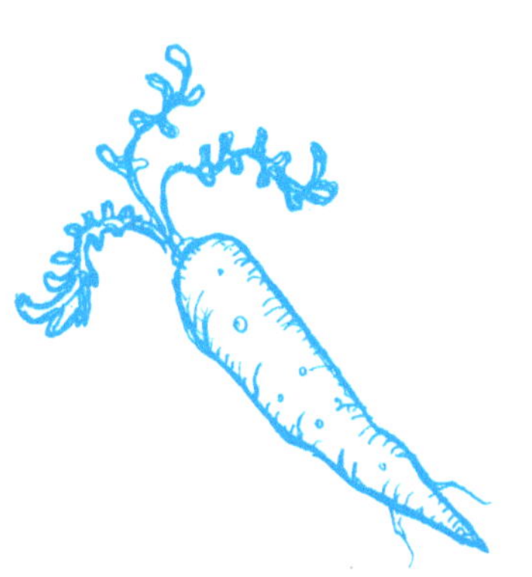

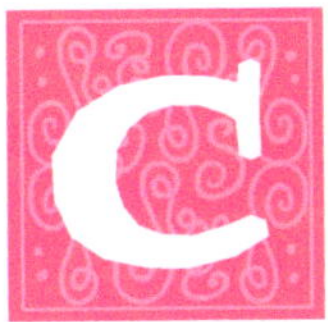 OOKING IS A POPULAR WAY TO MAKE DELICIOUS FOOD.

Yet, for too many, cooking is no fun. And food can be confusing, even for experienced eaters.

Oh, don't be sad. I am here to tell you that posh and fancy cooking does not need to be a chore. In fact, it's easier than you may think! Quite true.

I tell you simply, none of the recipes in this magnificent **Kitchen Workbook** are terribly difficult. They just require a little time, attention and love. Anyone can do. Be inspired by that! Are you hungry? Yes.

ON INGREDIENTS & ACCOUTREMENTS
This book is formatted with ingredients listed in the order used. The first time one is mentioned, it will appear in **pink**. The first time a necessary tool is mentioned, it will appear in **blue**. I'm afraid I must insist!

ON TECHNIQUE
You may have heard the French term **mis en place**. It simply refers to your cooking setup. The recipes in this book are written so that you automatically create your dishes using a *mis en place* technique. *Très simple!* Be sure to read each recipe thoroughly before starting, lest you find that you are not equipped to *brûlée* your *crème*. I tell you sweetly.

ON THE ASPECIFIC NATURE OF TRUE COOKING
In many cases, this book uses rather relativistic measurements. A recipe is an idea, not a formula! I encourage you to **use your own judgement**. If something seems too much or too little, adjust it! Otherwise, you're not even really cooking, I don't think.

ON GREAT MINDS
I have somehow convinced the greatest culinary minds from the esteemed faculty at **Frosting University** to guide you through each marvelous dish!

LASTLY
I would like to remind you that I am an anthropomorphic confection. Ho-ho!

Enjoy this book very much.

— Josiah

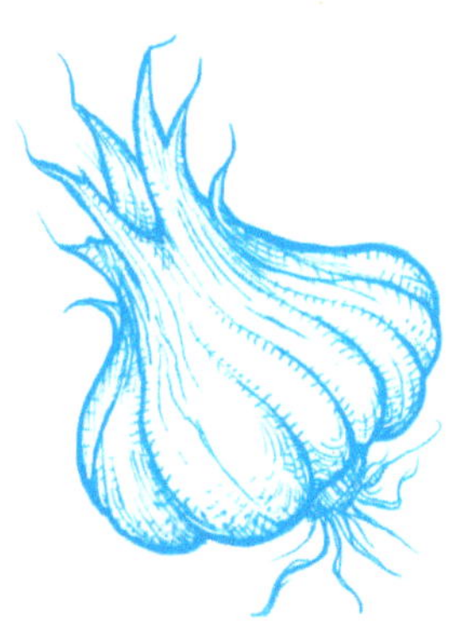

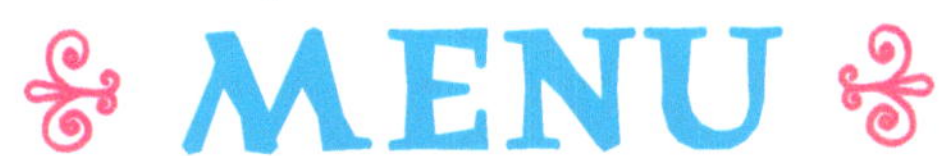 MENU

ENTRÉES

ROAST CHICKEN GF
with SEMPLO CABBAGE ... 13

BOEUF BOURGUIGNON GF
with BERGAMOT LEMON...15

CHICKEN SOUP
with BEDULAN METRINCTUS...17

SLOW-GRILLED CHICKEN GF
with JOSEPH BABIES...19

PASTA BOLOGNESE
with CIPOLLA PICCOLA ... 21

SIDES & STAPLES

RED CABBAGE SLAW GF, V
with ACORNICUS ... 25

MARINARA SAUCE GF, VG
with HOHO ... 27

MEATBALLS
with DRUSILLA TORSK ... 29

POTATOES AU GRATIN GF, V
with CARDAMOM ALEUTIAN BINGO ... 31

FRIJOLES DE LA OLLA GF, V, VG
with ARTHUR WRINKLES ... 33

SWEETS

CRÈME BRÛLÉE GF, V
with PORG CHOB ... 37

CHOCOLATE BREAD PUDDING V
with THEODORA OF BYZANTIUM ... 39

PISTACHIO ICE CREAM GF, V
with CURLINGTON THEWS ... 41

APPLE PIE V
with GLEPST FREEMLY ... 43

FROSTING'S CUPPYCAKES V
with JOSIAH FROSTING ... 45

LAZY MEALS

THE SANDWICH *can be* GF, V, VG
with TUREKY ... 49

SPAGHETTI ALLA PARMIGIANA V
with DINKUS PODAMES ... 51

CHICKEN SALAD WITH SOY DRESSING GF
with PIPSON GOURDE ... 53

BASIL PESTO GF, V
with CHUCKIE PIVENS ... 55

DO NOT ATTEMPT

HEAVY BALCH V ... 59
CABBAGE *with* **STIFLING GRAVIES** ... 61
THE HOMUNCULUS *can be* GF, V, VG... 63

APPENDIX

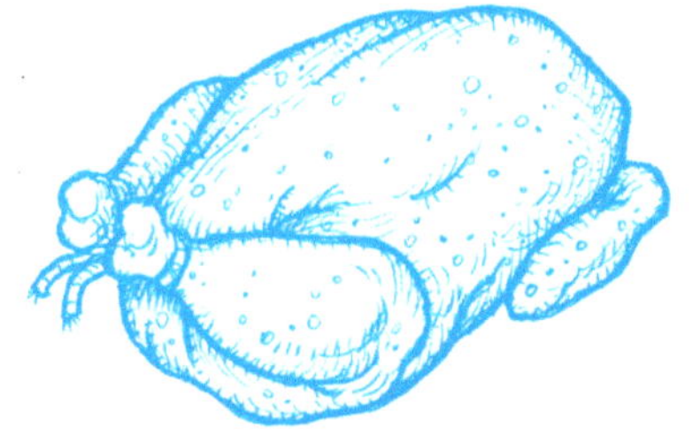

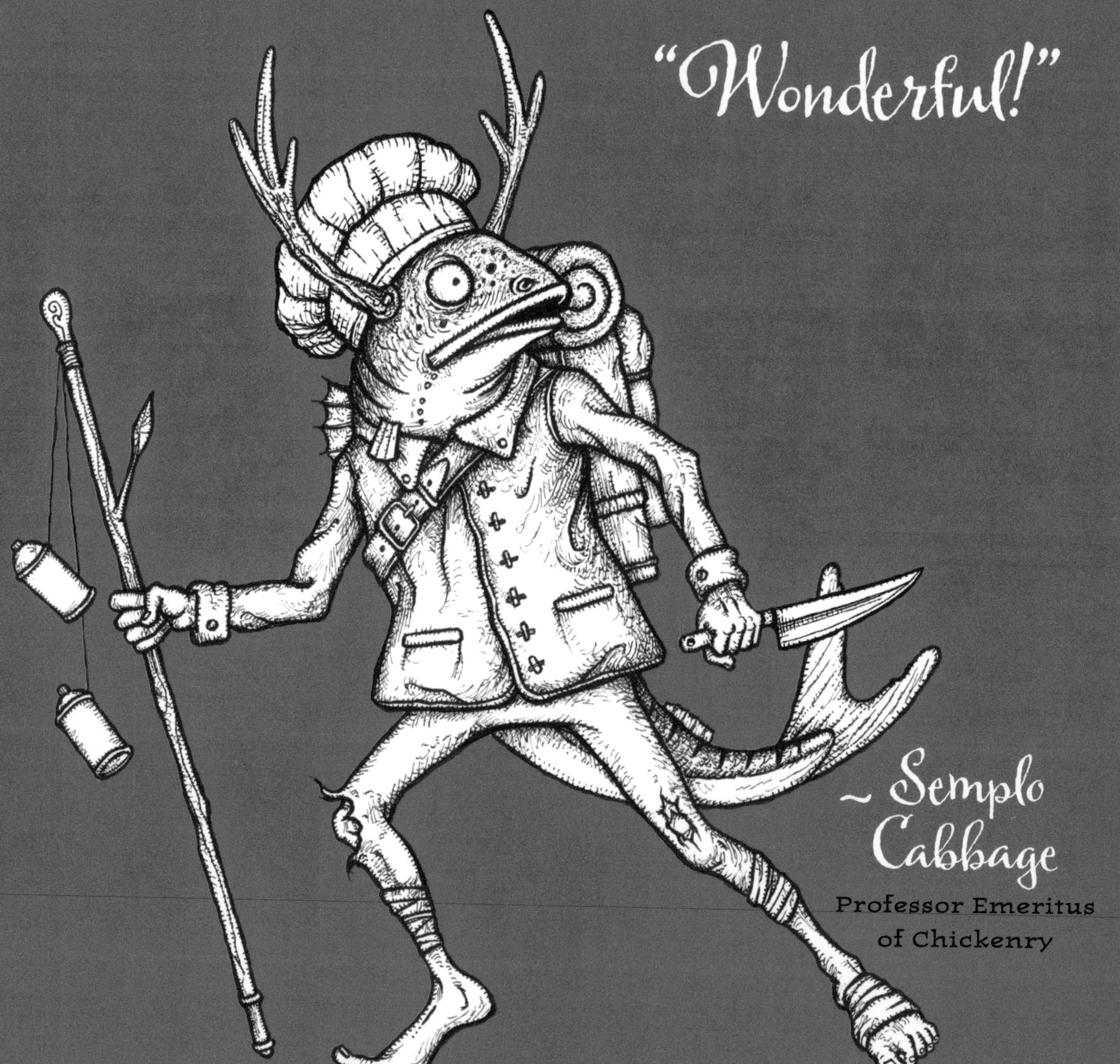

"Wonderful!"
~ Semplo Cabbage
Professor Emeritus of Chickenry

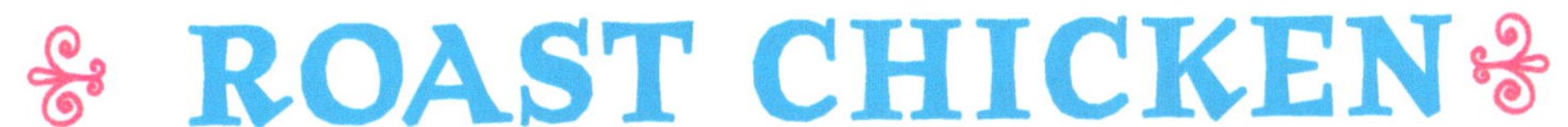
ROAST CHICKEN

Judiciously Buttered and Judgmatically Salted and Peppered • Serves 4 • **GF**

½ Onion • ½ Lemon • 3 Tablespoons Fresh Herbs (Thyme and/or Rosemary)
Additional Sprig of Thyme and/or Rosemary • 2 Pats of Cold Butter
One 4 Pound Chicken • Olive Oil
Two More Pats of Butter For Melting • Salt • Pepper

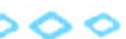

- Set up your oven to accommodate your roasting pan with rack. Pre-heat oven to 400 °.

- Halve an onion and a lemon. Set aside.

- Finely chop your thyme and/or rosemary and sprinkle one third over your two pats of cold butter. Set the herbed butter pats and remaining herbs aside.

- Dry chicken with a paper towel, inside and out, then place breast-side up on the rack of your roasting pan. You'll want to point the legs toward the back of the oven (which tends to be the hottest part), so make sure it's facing the right way in your pan.

- Insert your finger between the skin and breast meat on each side to make room for your herbed butter pats. Place one herbed pat under the skin on each side. Add lemon, onion and thyme and/or rosemary sprig to interior cavity of chicken.

- Rotate the wing tips toward the bird and tuck them under the wings. Tie the legs together at the bone end with some kitchen twine. Your chicken should look like a very compact sort of poultry grenade, see illustration on Page 10. This step helps keep your chicken breast moist.

- Wash your hands! This helps to prevent salmonella.

- In a small glass bowl or ramekin, melt two pats of butter in the microwave, then add some olive oil to the melted butter. Using a basting brush, coat the chicken all over with the butter and oil mixture.

- Generously salt and pepper the chicken. Sprinkle the remaining herbs over the chicken.

- Place immediately in the oven, with the legs of the chicken facing the back of the oven.

- Roast for 30 minutes, then reduce heat to 350 °. Roast for 30 more minutes, then rotate the roasting pan 180 °. Roast for another 30 minutes. (That's 90 minutes so far.)

- Test for doneness by inserting a meat thermometer into the thickest part of the breasts and the thighs. You want to reach 165 °. The thighs and legs cook faster than the breast, so if they read a little hotter, that's OK, they can take it! If needed, add time in 10 minute increments.

- When done, rest for 20 minutes on a cutting board with a drip groove, then carve and serve with potatoes and your favorite vegetable!

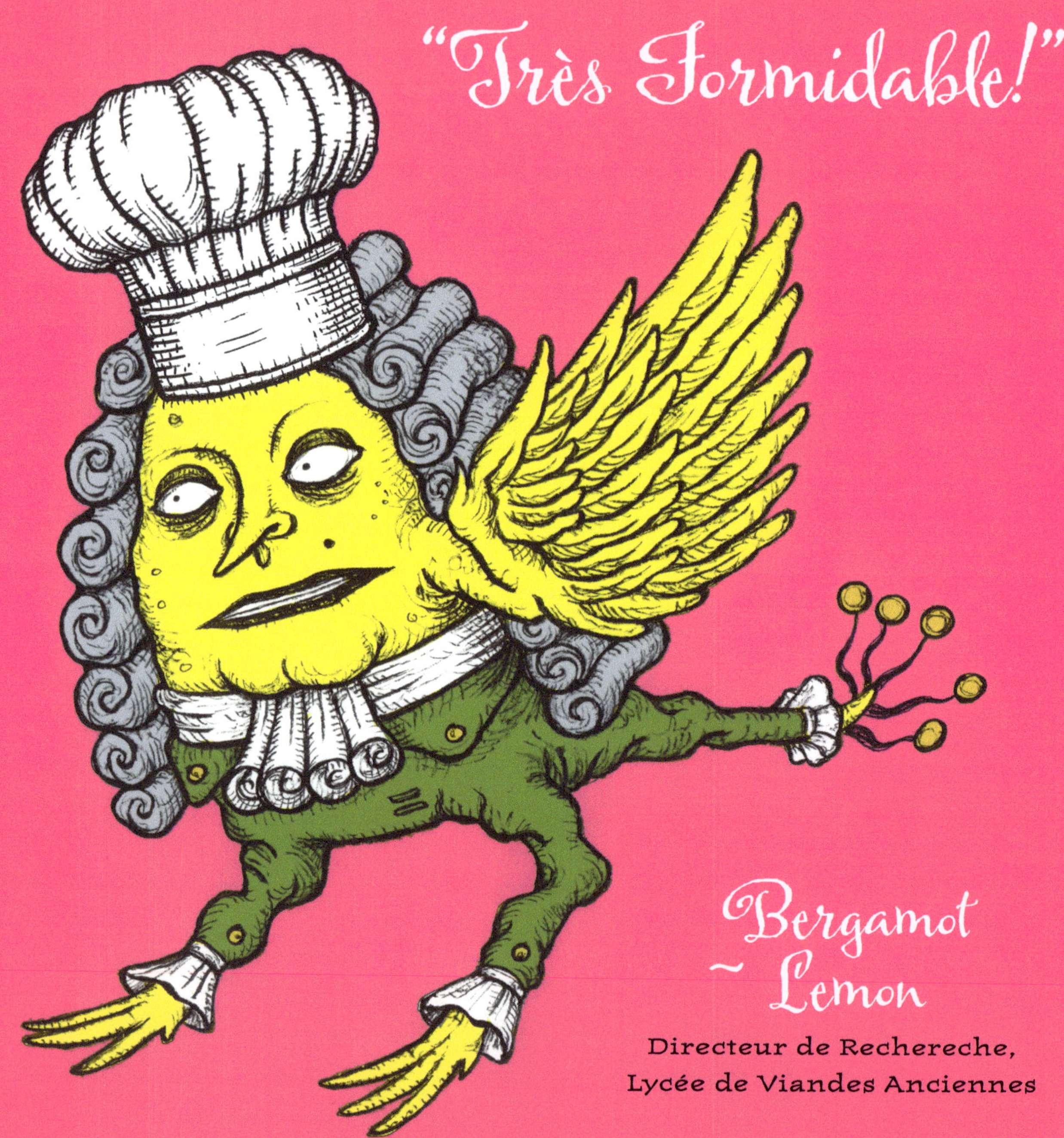

"Très Formidable!"
Bergamot
~ Lemon
Directeur de Rechereche,
Lycée de Viandes Anciennes

BOEUF BOURGUIGNON

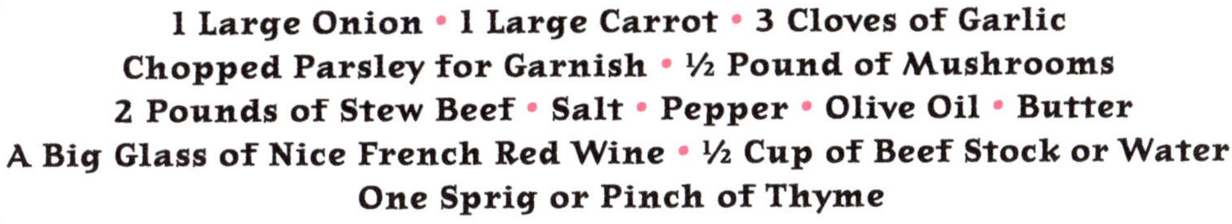

French-Style Beef Stew • Serves 4

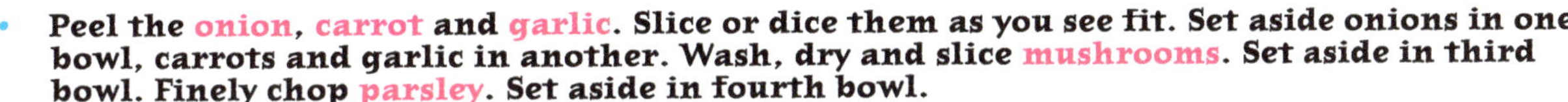

**1 Large Onion • 1 Large Carrot • 3 Cloves of Garlic
Chopped Parsley for Garnish • ½ Pound of Mushrooms
2 Pounds of Stew Beef • Salt • Pepper • Olive Oil • Butter
A Big Glass of Nice French Red Wine • ½ Cup of Beef Stock or Water
One Sprig or Pinch of Thyme**

- Peel the onion, carrot and garlic. Slice or dice them as you see fit. Set aside onions in one bowl, carrots and garlic in another. Wash, dry and slice mushrooms. Set aside in third bowl. Finely chop parsley. Set aside in fourth bowl.

- Dry beef with a paper towel, trim excess fat if necessary, then season on all sides with salt and pepper. Set aside. Remember to wash your hands after handling raw meat.

- In a gently pre-heated Dutch oven or large sautée pan, add a generous amount of olive oil. When oil is heated, add a pat of butter. Once the butter has melted, stir it into the olive oil using a wooden spatula.

- Brown beef on all sides, using tongs to turn beef. Increase heat a bit, if needed. Cook beef in batches if necessary, do not crowd pan. Transfer browned beef to a plate and set aside.

- Cook onions in the same pan until soft and translucent, about 5-7 minutes.

- Add wine, scraping any browned bits from bottom of pan with the wooden spatula (this is called deglazing). Bring to a boil to cook out the alcohol, then reduce to a simmer.

- Add the browned beef (along with any juices) and just enough beef stock or water so that only the top third of the beef is visible, as if they were little islands. Bring to a simmer.

- Add carrots, garlic and thyme. Stir to combine. Season with a bit more salt and pepper. Simmer low and cover.

- In separate pan, sautée mushrooms in olive oil and butter until they have given off their moisture, about 10 minutes. Add mushrooms to beef mixture and replace cover.

- Stir occasionally. Cook until beef is fork tender, about 3-4 hours. Adjust seasoning with salt and pepper if needed. Remove thyme branch if used. Using slotted spoon, serve beef over egg noodles or with mashed potatoes. Garnish with parsley.

NOTA BENE: If you substitute boneless skinless chicken thighs for the beef and reduce the cooking time by about one hour, you'll have Coq au Vin instead! Pas de problème!

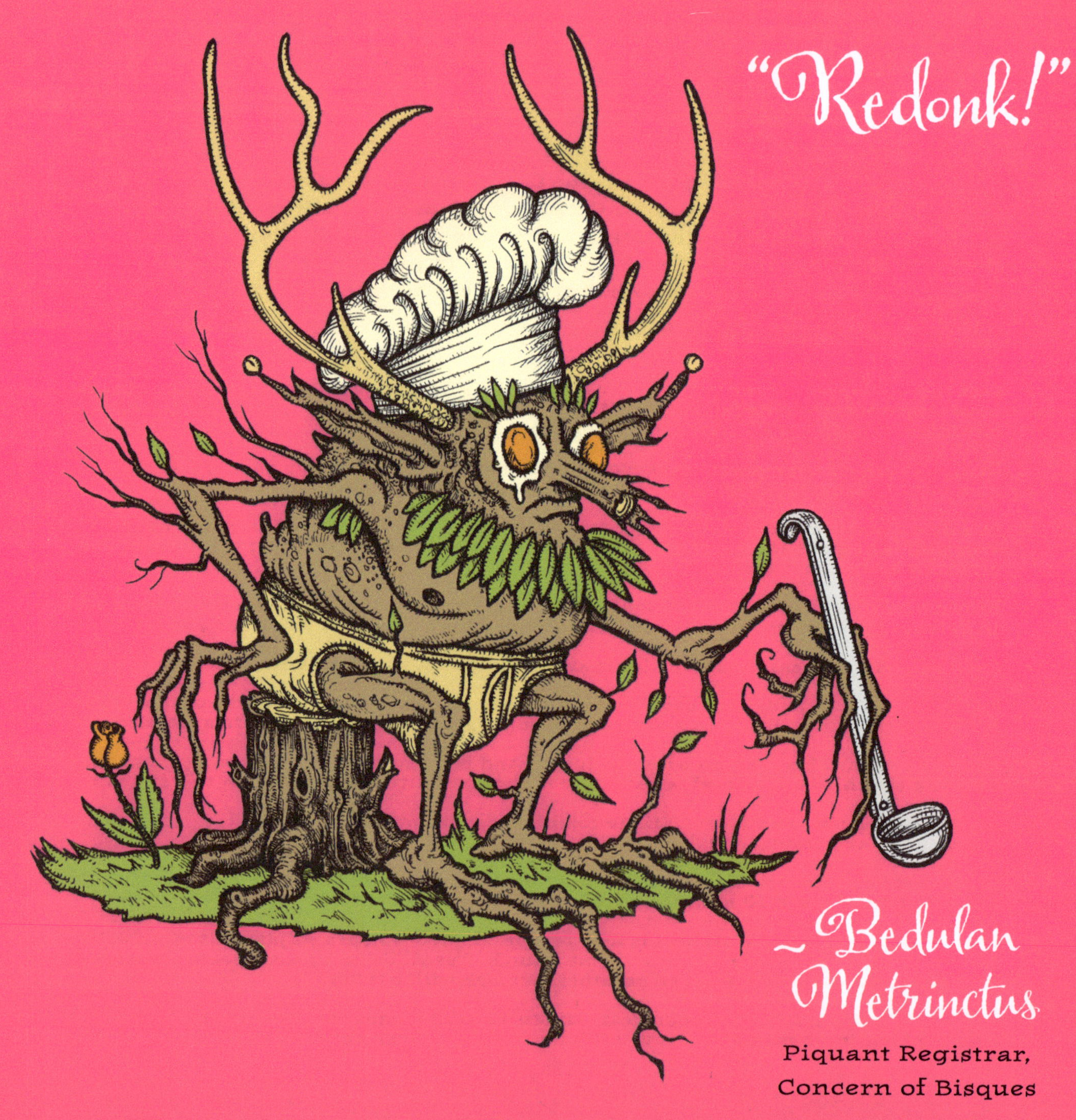

"Redonk!"
~ Bedulan
Metrinctus
Piquant Registrar,
Concern of Bisques

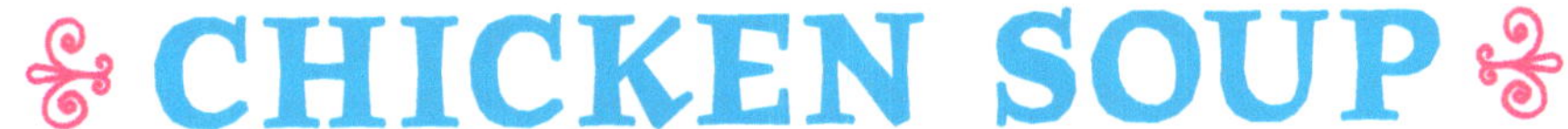

CHICKEN SOUP

Has Curative Properties • Serves 8

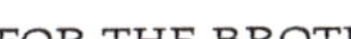

FOR THE BROTH
1 Large Onion • 1 Large Carrot • 2 Celery Stalks • 2 Garlic Cloves
2-3 Pounds of Chicken Scraps -or- 1 Small Whole Chicken • Water
Herb Mixture: Fresh or Dried Thyme, Oregano and Bay Leaf • Salt • Pepper
FOR THE SOUP
1 Large Onion • 1 Large Carrot • 2 Celery Stalks • 2 Cloves of Garlic
Broth • Reserved Chicken From Broth • Salt • Pepper • 2 Handfuls of Pasta
Fresh Parsley For Garnish

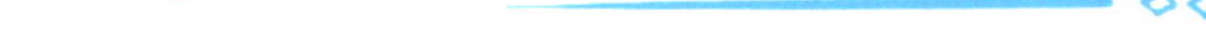

- Roughly chop an onion, a carrot, two celery stalks, and two garlic cloves (no need to peel!).

- Put chicken scraps (meat and bones leftover from previous meals) -or- a whole chicken into a large soup pot. Add the vegetables from the step above. Fill pot 80% full with cold water.

- Add the herb mixture to the pot. Add a generous amount of salt and pepper. If the pot seems too full, pour out some water so that it won't boil over.

- Bring just to a simmer and cook over medium-low heat for about 4 hours. Check periodically and reduce heat little by little as necessary. You'll get a clearer stock if the pot never comes to a boil, but it won't affect the flavor if it does boil.

- You have now made broth! Put a colander over a new pot and strain the broth. Retain hot bones, meat and veggies in colander and let cool for about an hour.

- Clean first pot and set a large mesh strainer over it. Working in batches, pour the broth into a fat separator, then through the mesh strainer until you've processed all of the broth. You can degrease manually by skimming or cooling, but what a chore!

- When cool, reserve the edible meat from the colander in a separate bowl. Compost the rest.

- When you're ready to make the final soup, re-heat the broth until it's rather hot.

- Peel the additional onion, carrot and garlic. Finely chop or dice these along with the celery and parsley. Add all but the parsley to the broth and cook at medium heat until the onions are translucent, about 10 minutes. Add the reserved chicken from step above.

- Add pasta (broken spaghetti or whatever you like) and cook until al dente, maybe 10 minutes. Remove from heat. Adjust seasoning if necessary. Let cool for 5 minutes, garnish with fresh parsley and serve in big soup bowls.

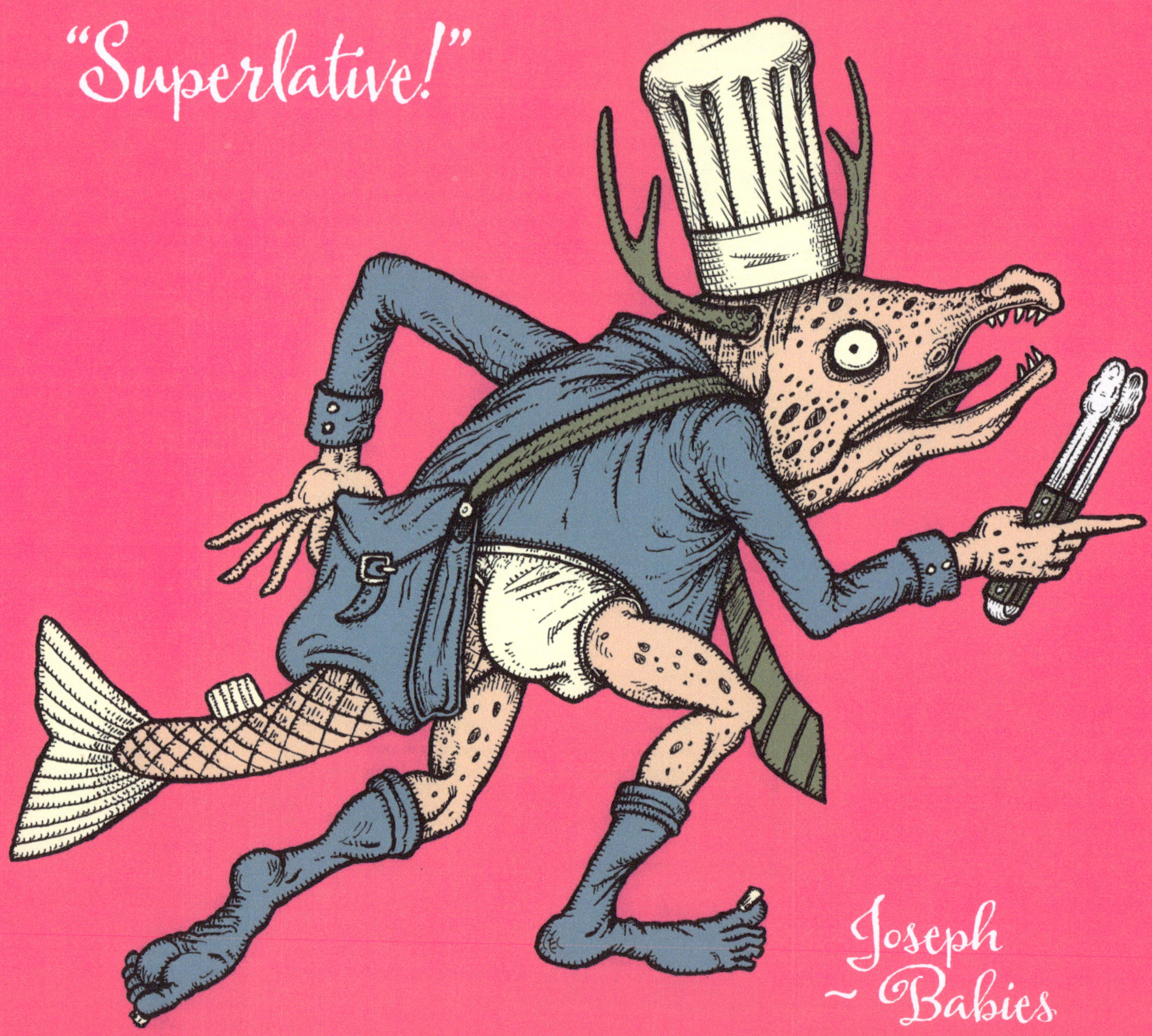
"Superlative!"
Joseph
~ Babies
Endowed Chair Professor,
Conservatory of Vinegars

SLOW-GRILLED CHICKEN

A Fragrant Fowl • Serves 4 • GF

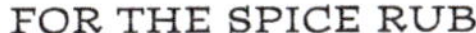

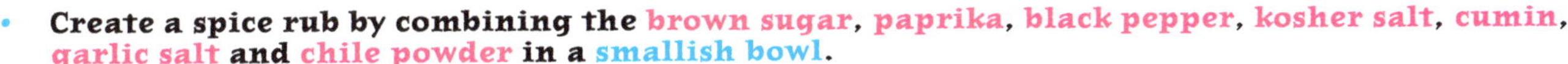

FOR THE SPICE RUB
¼ Cup of Brown Sugar • ¼ Cup of Paprika • 2 Tablespoons Ground Black Pepper
4 Tablespoons Kosher Salt • 1 Tablespoon Ground Cumin • 1 Tablespoon Garlic Salt
1 Tablespoon Ancho Chile Powder
FOR THE MOP
½ Cup of Apple Cider Vinegar • A Few Slices of Onion • Pinch of Salt • Pinch of Pepper
Pinch of Red Pepper Flakes
AND DON'T FORGET
One 4-5 Pound Chicken • Commercial BBQ Sauce

- Create a spice rub by combining the brown sugar, paprika, black pepper, kosher salt, cumin, garlic salt and chile powder in a smallish bowl.

- Cut a few slices of onion. Create a mop sauce by combining the onion, vinegar, salt, pepper and red pepper flakes in another smallish bowl. This sauce will help keep your chicken moist over a long, slow cook.

- Spatchcock your chicken by cutting out its backbone with kitchen shears! Start snipping up from the tail and cut all the way to the neck. Do this on both sides of the spine. Place breast side up on a baking sheet and flatten it out a bit. Remember to wash your hands each time you handle raw poultry.

- Generously sprinkle the spice rub over both sides of the chicken, then rub it into the skin. Any extra spice rub can be kept in an airtight container for three months or more.

- Set up your charcoal grill for indirect grilling. Place two sets of hot coals on the right and left sides of your grill, then place an aluminum drip pan between the coals. Replace the grilling grate and let your grill reach a moderate temperature (about 300°).

- Use long BBQ tongs to place the chicken in the center of the grill, over the aluminum pan. Watch for flareups and move the chicken if necessary. Place the lid on your grill and monitor the temperature, adding coals when needed, but letting the heat stay moderate to low (shoot for about 250°).

- Every 30 minutes, use a basting brush to coat the chicken generously with the mop sauce.

- Grill the chicken for about 2 hours. Add more coals as needed. Brush lightly with BBQ sauce about 10 minutes before it's ready. Chicken is done when the thigh meat reaches 165° on a meat thermometer. Other ways to determine doneness are when the juices run clear (not pinkish), and/or when the legs wiggle freely.

- Rest for 10-15 minutes on a cutting board with a drip groove, then carve and serve with Red Cabbage Slaw (Page 25) and Frijoles de la Olla (Page 33)!

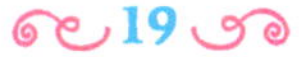

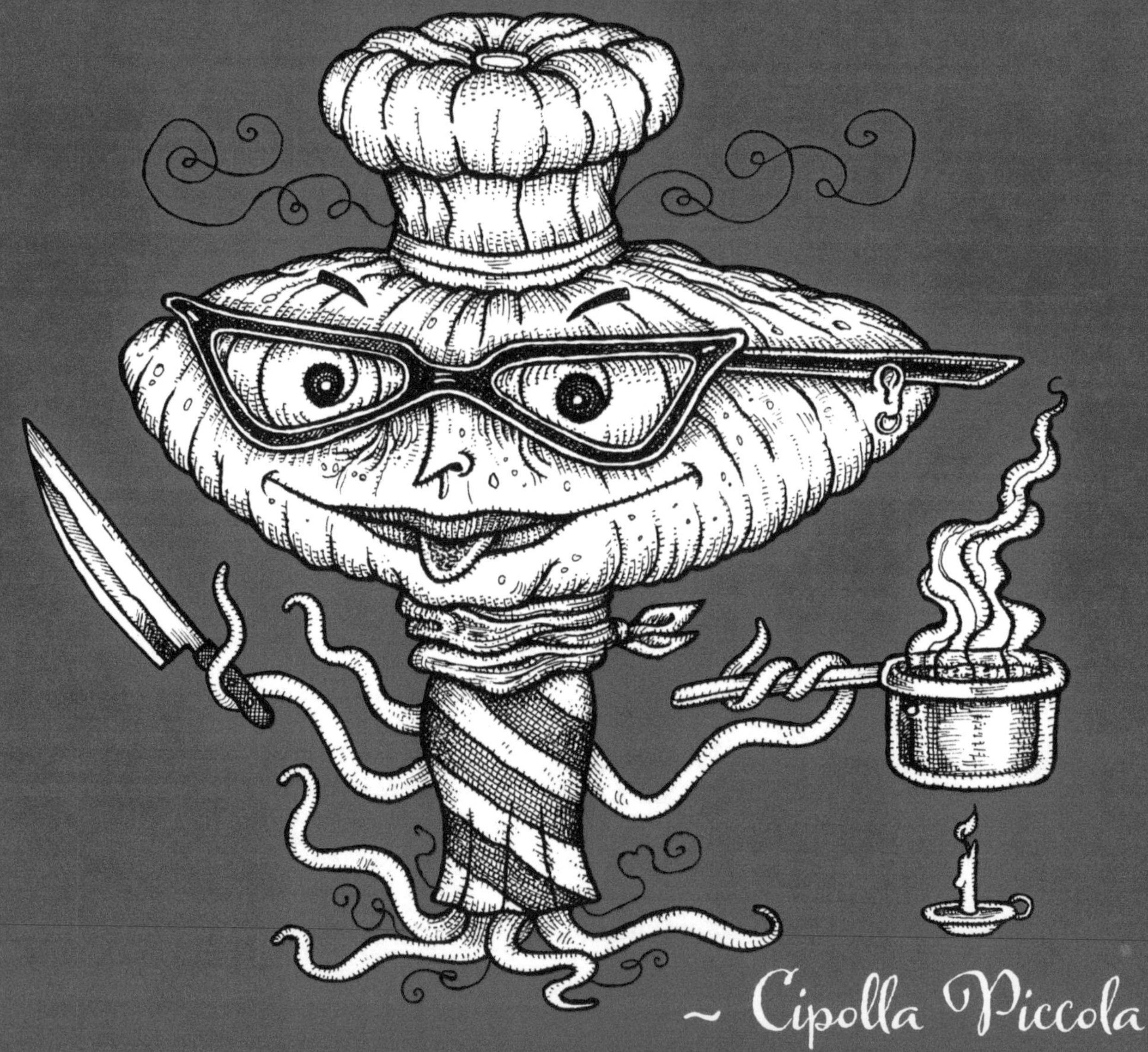

"Molto Buono!"
~ Cipolla Piccola
Adjunct Professoressa,
Academy of the Low Simmer

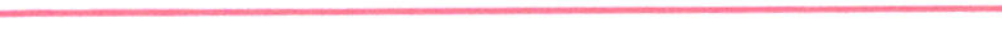

✦ PASTA BOLOGNESE ✦

Classic Italian Ragù • Serves 4-6

1 Large Onion • 1 Large Carrot • 2 Garlic Cloves • 2 Celery Stalks
Parsley for Garnish • ½ Pound of Ground Pork • ½ Pound of Ground Veal –or– Ground Beef
Olive Oil • Salt • Pepper • 2 Ounces Pancetta • About 2 Tablespoons Tomato Paste
Half A Glass of Nice Italian White Wine • ½ Cup of Milk • 1 Cup of Marinara Sauce
2 Sprigs or Pinches of Thyme • Package of Tagliatelle or Other Pasta
Imported Parmigiano-Reggiano Cheese

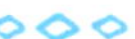

- Peel the onion, carrot and garlic. Finely chop or dice them along with the celery. Set aside onions, carrots and celery in one bowl, garlic in another. Finely chop parsley. Set aside in a third bowl.

- In a gently pre-heated medium-to-large sauce pot, add a generous amount of olive oil. When oil is heated, cook the onion, carrot and celery until soft, about 8 minutes. Lightly season with salt and pepper.

- In the same pot, add the ground pork and veal (–or– beef), and cook until browned, about 8 minutes. Lightly season with salt and pepper.

- Add in the pancetta and cook for a few minutes. Squeeze in the tomato paste and cook for a few minutes more. Add the garlic and cook for a few minutes more.

- Add the wine and milk. Bring to boil to cook out the alcohol, then reduce to simmer.

- Add the marinara sauce (Page 27, or use ready-made). Bring to simmer. Add the thyme.

- Cover and cook at a simmer for 2-3 hours, stirring occasionally. Taste and adjust seasoning as needed.

- Cook pasta in generously salted water per package directions. Remove thyme branch from sauce if used. Drain pasta and add most of the sauce to it, coating thoroughly. Add some more pepper and a generous amount of grated Parmigiano-Reggiano cheese. Stir to combine.

- Top with a little more sauce. Garnish with parsley and serve with a generous additional amount of grated Parmigiano-Reggiano cheese (don't skimp, accept no substitutes!) and a bottle of DOCG Valpolicella.

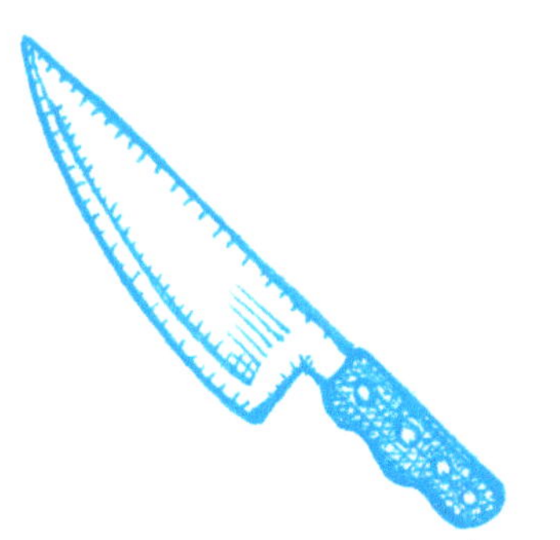

SIDES & STAPLES

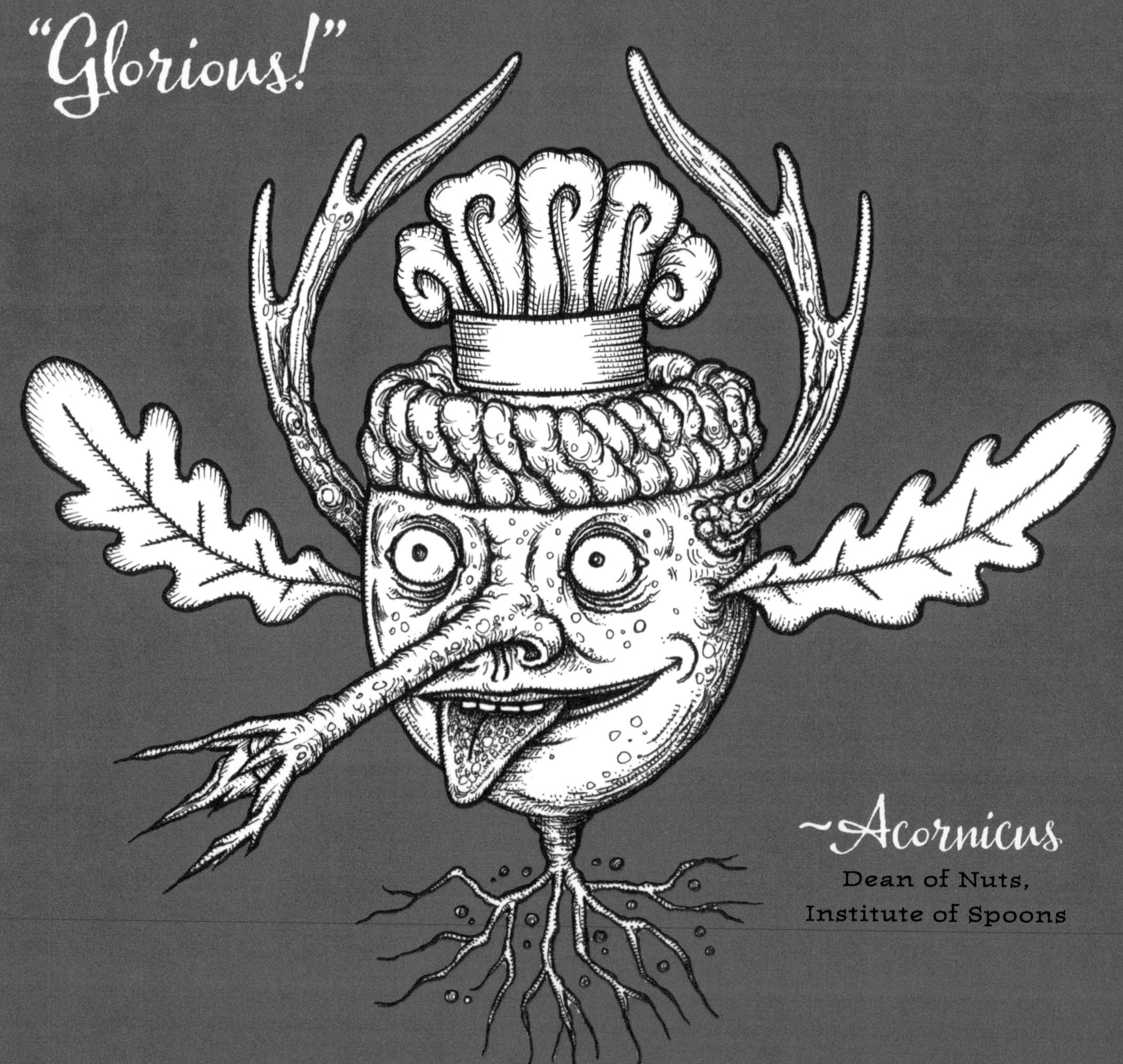
"Glorious!"
~Acornicus
Dean of Nuts,
Institute of Spoons

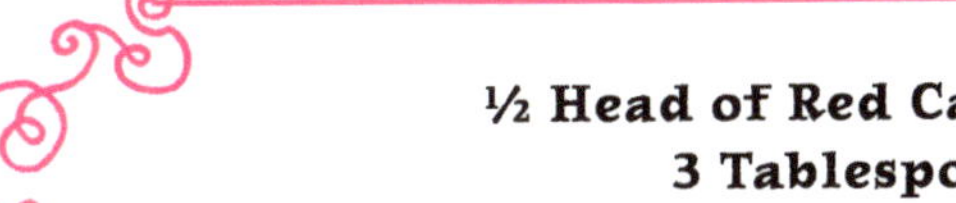# RED CABBAGE SLAW

A Stonking Summertime Salmagundi • Serves 4-6 • **GF, V**

½ Head of Red Cabbage • 1 Carrot • ½ Red Onion
3 Tablespoons White Wine Vinegar
3 Tablespoons Avocado –or– Other Salad Oil
2 Tablespoons Dijon Mustard • 3 Tablespoons Honey
Salt • Pepper • 1 Tablespoon Poppy Seeds

- Finely shred cabbage with a long, sharp knife and place in a large bowl.

- Finely chop or dice onion. Cut carrot into julienne strips or shred using a grater. Add to bowl with cabbage.

- Make a dressing by combining the vinegar, salad oil, mustard and honey. Adjust ingredients to suit your palate. Lightly whisk together.

- Pour dressing mixture into bowl with cabbage, onion and carrots. Add poppy seeds, salt and pepper. Stir to combine thoroughly. Taste and adjust seasoning if needed.

- Cover bowl and let stand in the refrigerator for 2-3 hours. You're essentially lightly pickling the cabbage mixture, so the flavor will change a bit as time passes. Taste and adjust seasoning again if needed.

- Serve with Slow-Grilled Chicken (Page 19), or with just about any barbecued dish. Also great on top of tacos! Leftover slaw will keep for 3-4 days if tightly covered.

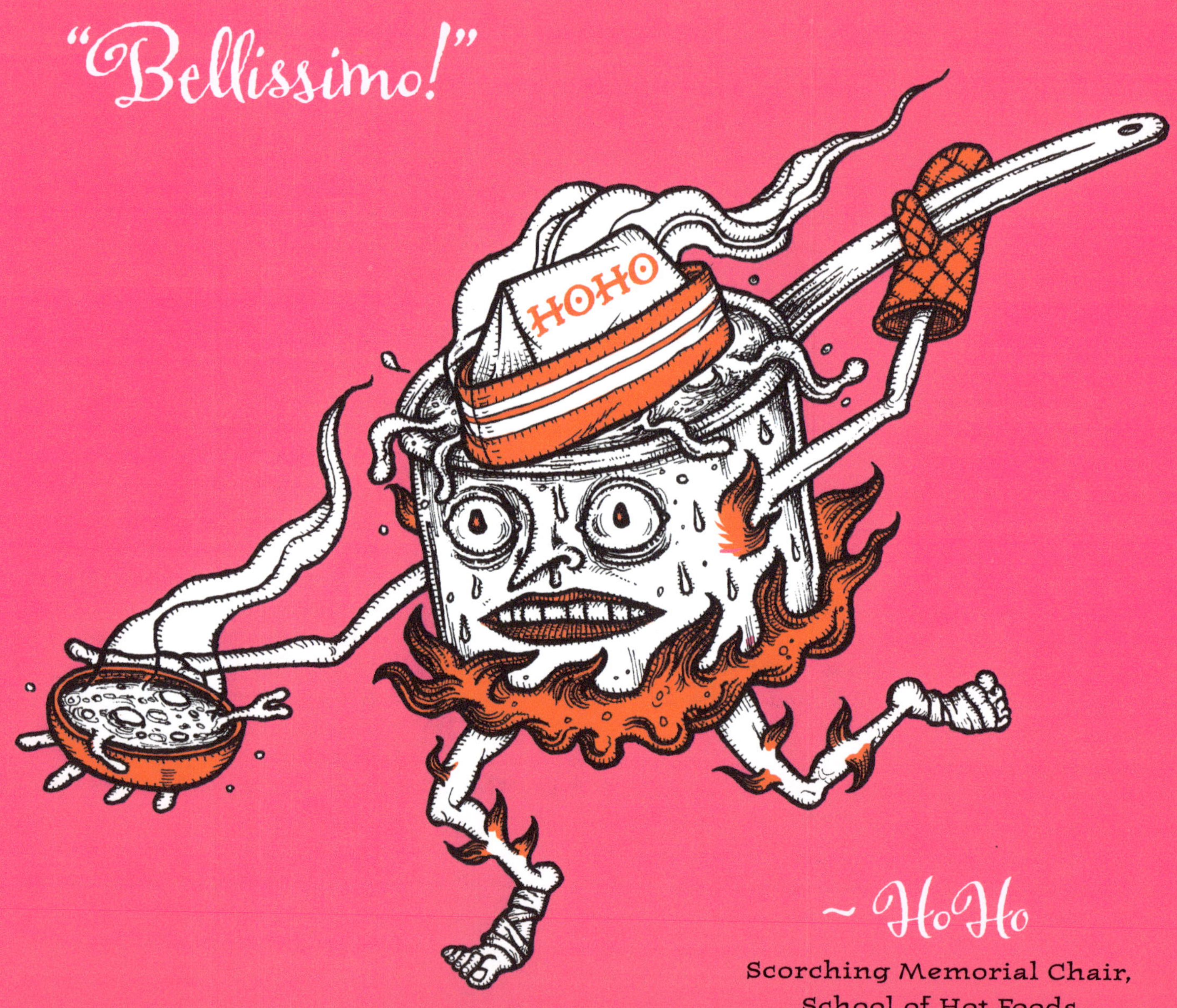

"Bellissimo!"
HOHO
~ HoHo
Scorching Memorial Chair,
School of Hot Foods

MARINARA SAUCE

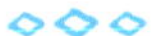

Sunday Gravy • Serves 6-8 • **GF, V, VG**

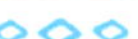

1 Large Onion • 1 Large Carrot • 2 Garlic Cloves • 2 Celery Stalks
Three 18 oz. -or- Two 28 oz. Cans of Imported DOP San Marzano Tomatoes
Olive Oil • Salt • Pepper • About 2 Tablespoons Tomato Paste
A Glass of Nice Chianti • 1 Bay Leaf • 1 Sprig or Pinch of Thyme

- Peel the onion, carrot and garlic. Finely chop or dice them along with the celery. Set aside onions, carrots and celery in one bowl, garlic in another.

- Crush the San Marzano tomatoes. Do it with your hands in a large bowl to make smaller pieces (fun!) -or- use a food processor -or- immersion blender for a smoother purée. You can use other types of canned tomatoes, but don't skimp - use the real thing.

- In a gently pre-heated medium-to-large sauce pot, add a generous amount of olive oil. When oil is heated, cook the onion, carrot and celery until soft, stirring occasionally, about 8 minutes. Lightly season with salt and pepper.

- Add in the garlic and stir. Cook for a few minutes, until fragrant. Add in the tomato paste and stir in thoroughly. Cook for a few minutes more. Lightly season with salt and pepper.

- Add the tomatoes, stir, increase heat and bring to a simmer.

- Add the Chianti. Stir and bring to boil to cook out the alcohol, then reduce to simmer.

- Add the bay leaf and thyme. If you like, add other herbs, such as oregano or basil. Lightly season with salt and pepper.

- Stir to combine. Simmer low and cover.

- Cook covered for 6-10 hours, stirring occasionally and adjusting for seasoning as necessary. If sauce seems too thin, turn up the heat a bit to cook out some of the liquid. For extra happiness, why not make some meatballs (Page 29)?

- When done, let sauce cool for 10 minutes, then serve with your favorite pasta. Leftover sauce (and meatballs) can be refrigerated for 5-6 days or frozen for 3 months in tightly sealed containers. Va bene!

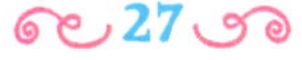

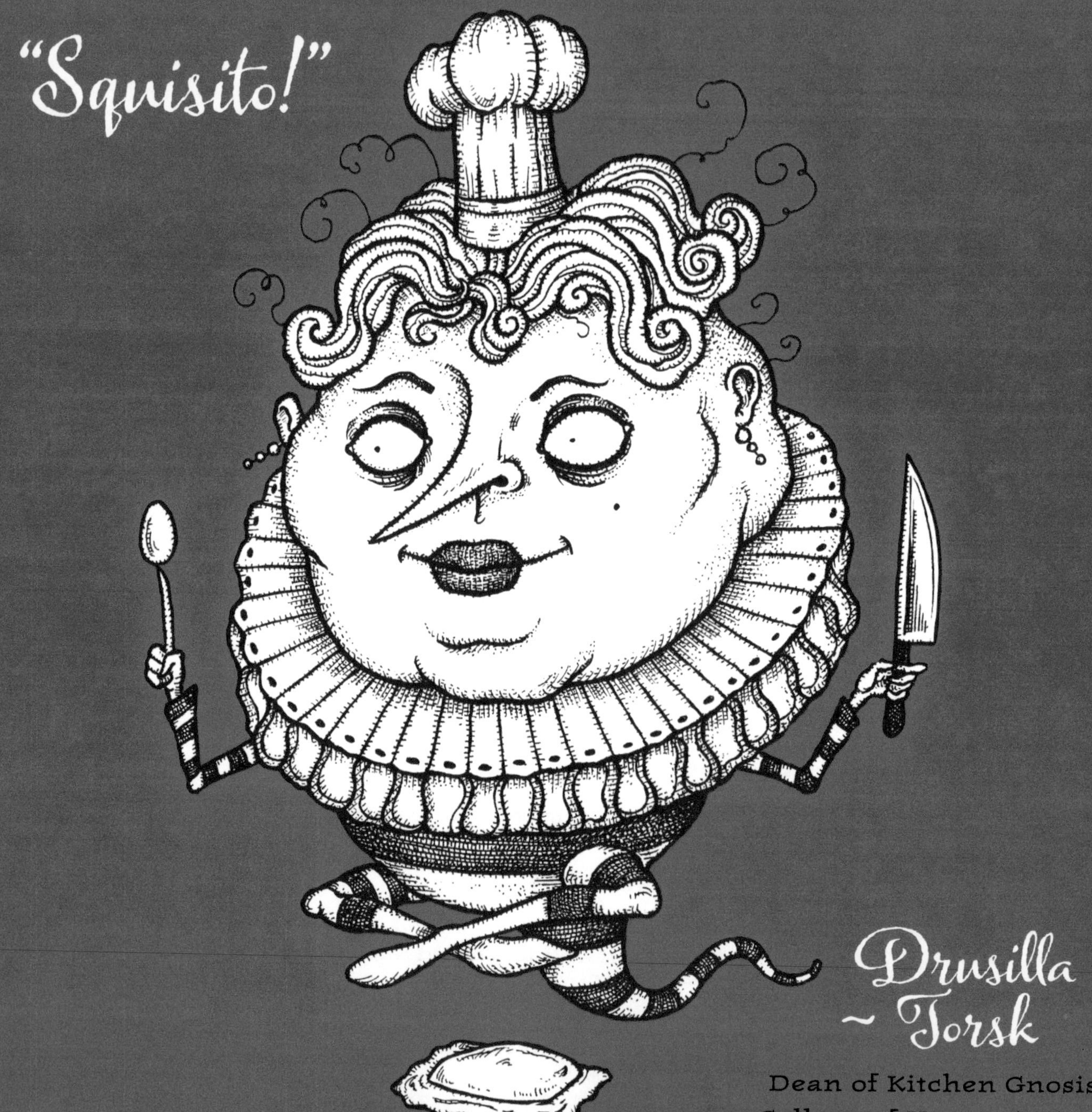

"Squisito!"
Drusilla
~ Torsk
Dean of Kitchen Gnosis,
College of Hermetic Seals

MEATBALLS

I Hear You Calling, Marinara • Serves 3-4

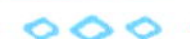

2 Whole Eggs • ½ Large Onion • 1 Garlic Clove
2 Tablespoons Fresh Chives • Imported Parmigiano-Reggiano Cheese
2 Tablespoons Dry Italian Red Wine • Salt • Pepper • 1 Pound of Ground Pork
About 1 ½ Cups of Italian Breadcrumbs • Olive Oil

- Place a sautée pan on your stove, but don't heat it up just yet.

- Crack the two eggs into a large mixing bowl and whisk them together thoroughly.

- Peel the onion and garlic. Finely chop or dice them along with the chives and place them in the bowl with the eggs.

- Grate in a generous amount of the cheese, then add the wine, salt and pepper. Add in the pork and mix with your dominant hand to combine thoroughly. The idea is to only have one "dirty" hand at a time.

- Using your clean non-dominant hand, add in the breadcrumbs, combining with your "dirty" hand. The finished mixture should hold together rather well and not be too mushy.

- With your clean hand, turn on the heat to medium under your sautée pan and add a generous amount of olive oil. Bring your mixing bowl close to the pan.

- Using both hands, form the mixture into 8-10 golf-ball sized spheres, setting them gently in the oiled pan.

- Wash your hands! Using a slotted spoon, rotate a meatball when the bottom is browned – you'll know because it won't resist and stick to the pan. Do the same with the rest of the meatballs, and then continue until all sides have been browned, 8-10 minutes.

- Bring the sautée pan close to your warm uncovered marinara sauce (Page 27) and gently lower the meatballs in, being careful not to break them, and making sure they are submerged. Cook at a low simmer for at least one hour. –or– Drain the meatballs on paper towels and then bake on a cookie sheet at 350 ° for about 12-15 minutes, so that you're sure the centers are cooked.

- Serve with marinara sauce over pasta –or– make a toasted meatball grinder (Page 49) by adding marinara sauce and mozzarella cheese. Bake sandwich open-faced on a cookie sheet at 350 ° for about 10 minutes, or until the cheese just browns.

- NOTA BENE: You can use ground beef, veal, decased sausage, or even ground turkey instead of pork. Seasonings and herbs can also be adjusted to your tastes. Experiment!

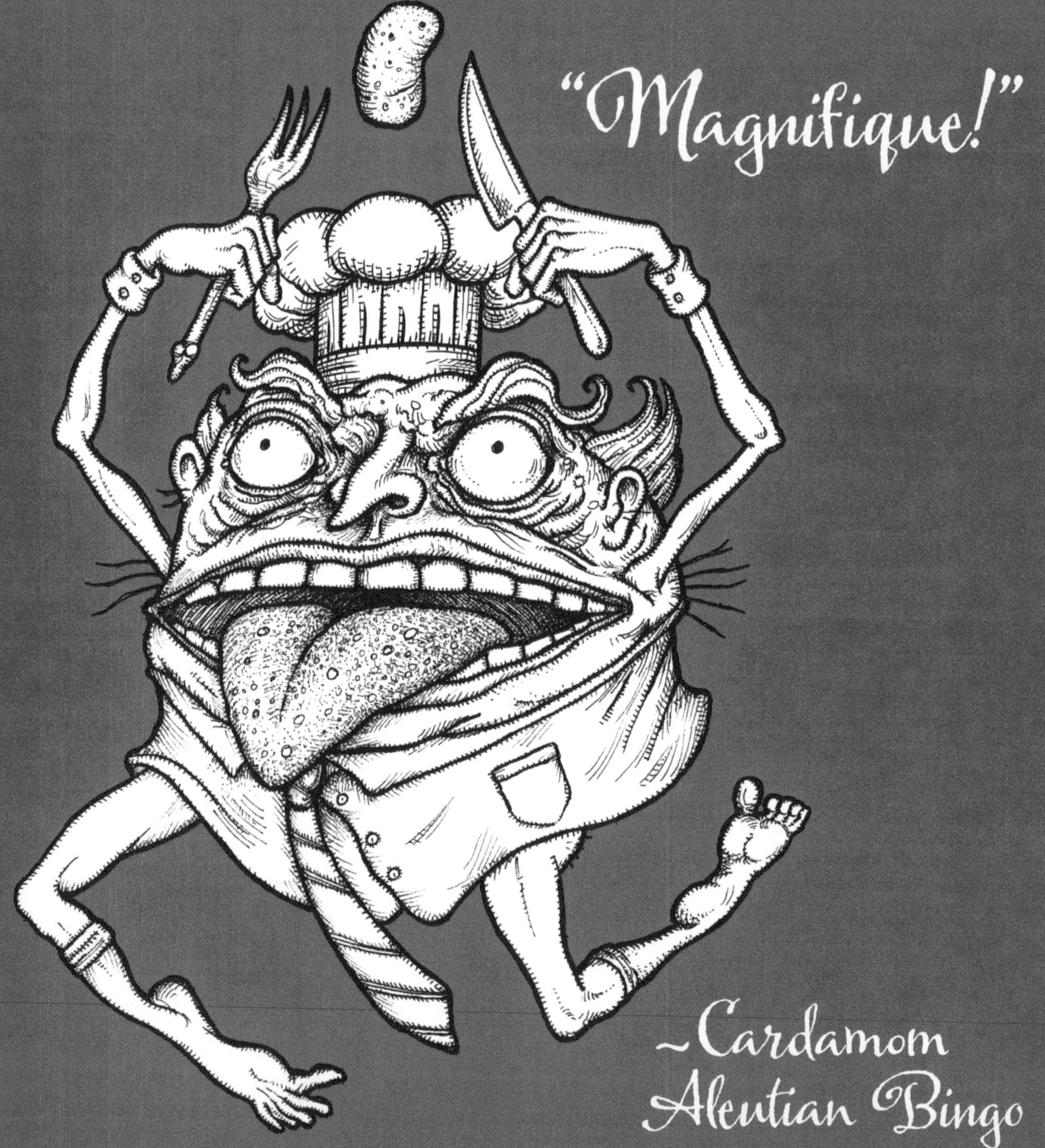
"Magnifique!"
~Cardamom
Aleutian Bingo
Faculty, Chewing Auditorium

POTATOES AU GRATIN

Wonderful Potatoes and Cheese • Serves 6–8 • **GF, V**

1 Clove of Garlic • 12 Ounces of Gruyère –or– Other Nice Cheese
3–4 Large Russet Potatoes
2 Tablespoons Butter, Plus A Bit More For the Baking Dish
1 ¼ Cups of Heavy Cream • Salt • Pepper

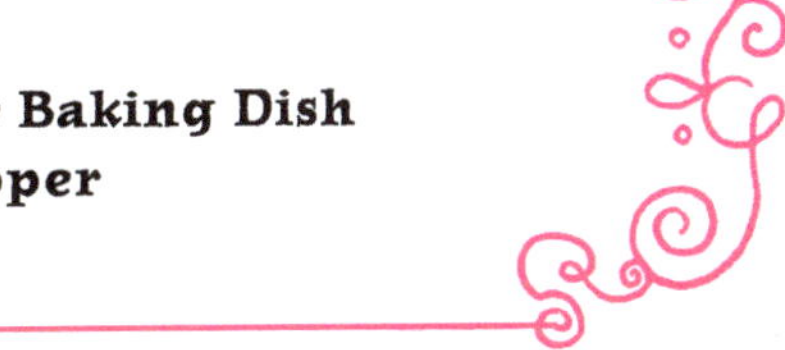

- Pre-heat oven to 400°.

- Peel and crush garlic and set aside in a small bowl.

- Grate, slice or tear up the cheese and set aside in another bowl.

- Wash and peel potatoes. Slice to about ⅛th inch thickness or thinner. If you have a mandoline slicer, great, otherwise it's pretty easy to cut the potato slices evenly enough.

- Rub butter over the bottom and sides of a square or oval flameproof baking dish, then rub it again with crushed garlic. Discard the garlic, or save it for another recipe.

- Arrange one layer of sliced potatoes in the baking dish, distribute ⅓ of the cheese over it, then lightly season with salt and pepper. Repeat two more times until you have three layers.

- In a small sauce pot, bring the cream and the remaining butter almost to a boil. Stir to combine and take the pan off the heat.

- Place the baking dish on a cookie sheet in case of spillage. Gently and evenly pour the hot cream and butter over the layers of potatoes and cheese.

- Bake 40–50 minutes until the top has browned, the potatoes are tender and the liquid is mostly absorbed. It will be lava-hot! Let it cool for 30 minutes, and then serve warm!

AN EXCURSUS ON CHEESE: Your results will be best when the cheese you use is of high-quality. Pricey imported Gruyère works the best, but excellent Swiss and domestic cheddar cheeses are also nice. Don't use pre-packaged sandwich cheese, it's sometimes oily and nasty when baked.

NOTA BENE: If you want to slice the potatoes a little ahead of time, you can place them in a bowl of acidulated water, which is simply water with a little vinegar or lemon juice added to prevent discoloring. Works great for apples, too! Just remember to dry your potatoes (or apples) thoroughly before using.

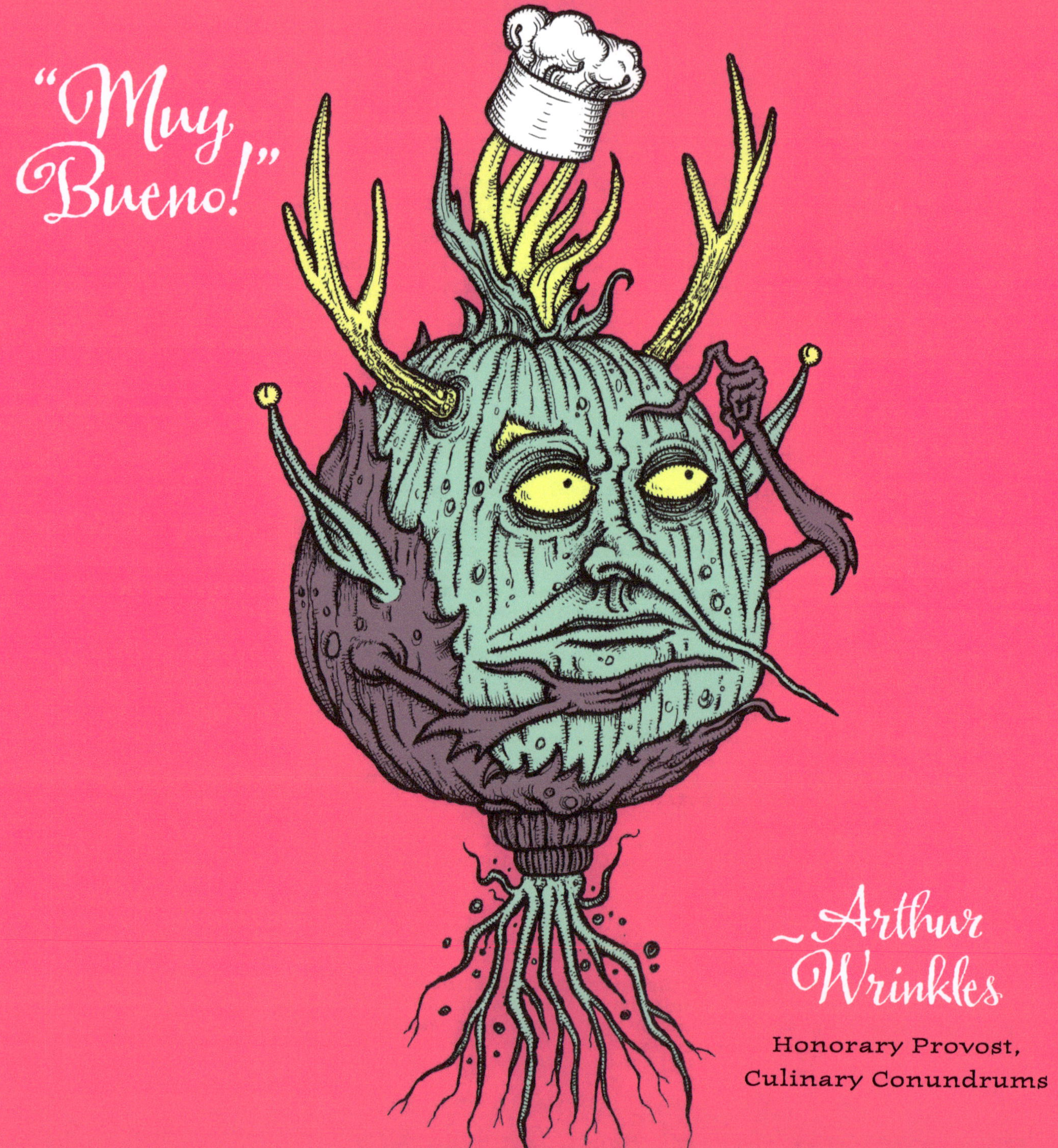

"Muy Bueno!"
~Arthur Wrinkles
Honorary Provost,
Culinary Conundrums

FRIJOLES DE LA OLLA

Mexican-Style Beans with Adobo • Serves 6-8 • GF, V, VG

FOR THE ADOBO SPICE MIXTURE
2 or 3 Dried Ancho and/or Pasillo Chiles • ¼ Cup of Cumin Seeds
¼ Cup of Coriander Seeds • ¼ Cup of Yellow Mustard Seeds • ¼ Cup of Fennel Seeds
2 Tablespoons Onion or Garlic Powder • ¼ Cup of Sweet or Hot Paprika
FOR THE BEANS
½ Small Onion • 2 Cloves of Garlic • 1 ½ Cups of Pinto or Black Beans
Water • Adobo • Salt • Pepper • Mexican Hot Sauce

- Seed and de-vein the dried peppers. Chop roughly or tear apart.

- In a hot non-stick skillet, place the peppers along with the cumin seeds, coriander seeds, yellow mustard seeds and fennel seeds. Toast until almost smoking, about 3-5 minutes. Shake the sautée pan now and again to prevent burning. Place on a large dinner plate and allow to cool completely.

- Add the toasted seeds and peppers to a spice grinder and pulverize. Work in two batches if necessary. Old coffee grinders (with the coffee cleaned out!) make great spice grinders.

- In a medium bowl, add the ground spices to the onion or garlic powder and the paprika. Combine thoroughly. You have now made adobo, a Mexican-style seasoning mixture!

- Roughly chop the onion and garlic.

- Add the beans to a medium saucepan and fill pot two-thirds with water. No need to soak the beans, seriously!

- Add chopped onion, garlic, a generous pinch or two of adobo, a generous pinch or two of salt, a bit of pepper and a few splashes of hot sauce to the pot. Bring to boil, cover and reduce to simmer. Check beans after 45 minutes to see if you need to add any more water.

- Cook at a simmer until the beans are tender, about 3-4 hours. Adjust seasoning if needed, drain off some of the excess water and serve with a slotted spoon! Store any extra adobo in an airtight container for up to 3 months.

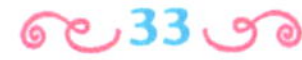

SWEETS

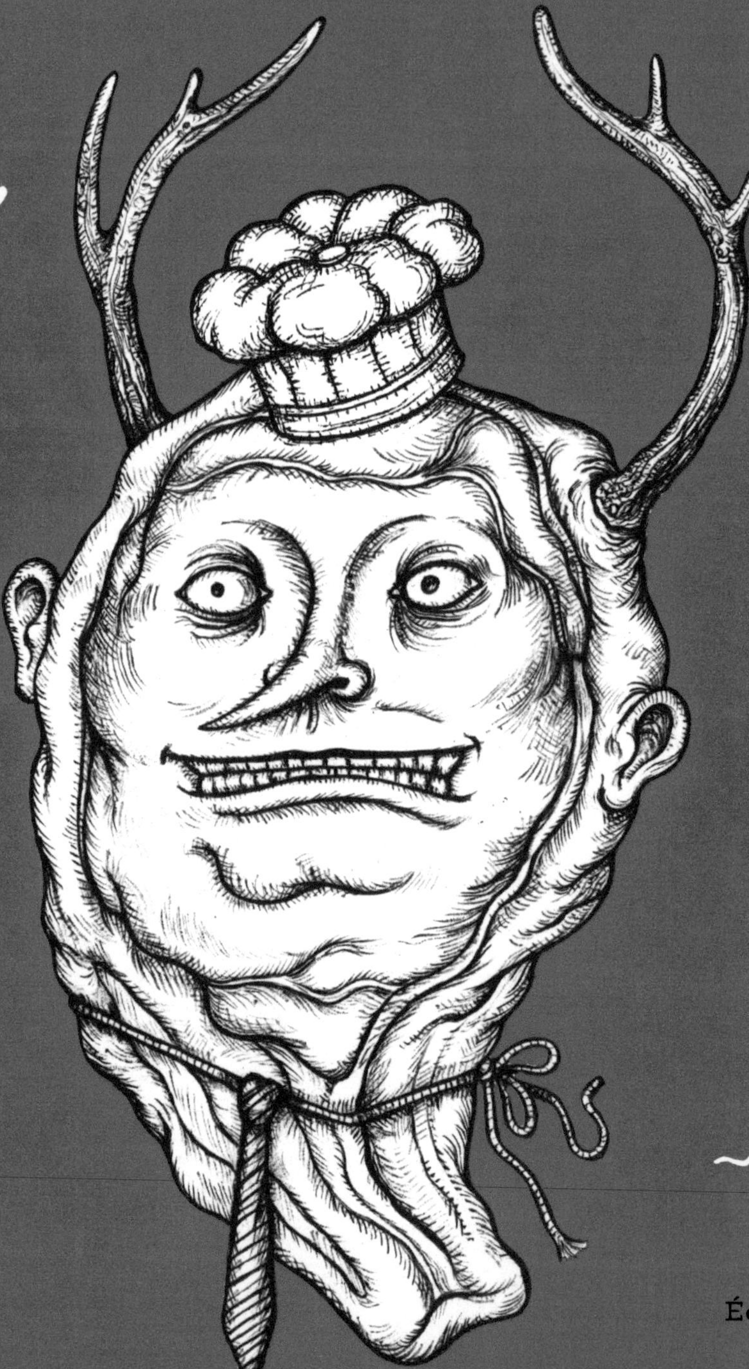

"Très Bon!"
~ Porg Chob
Pâtissier,
École de Porc

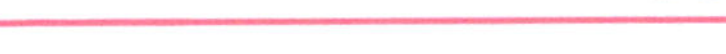
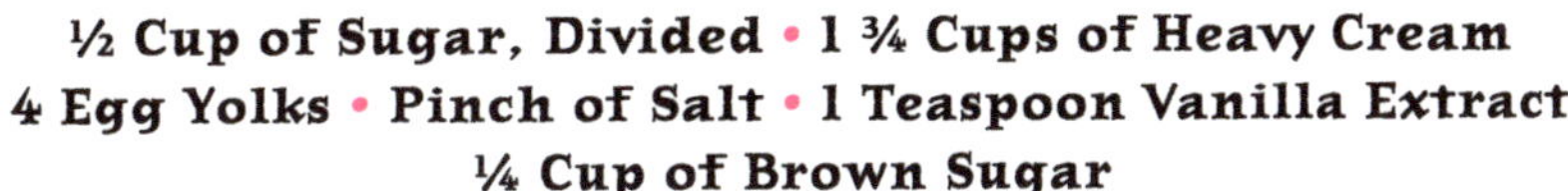
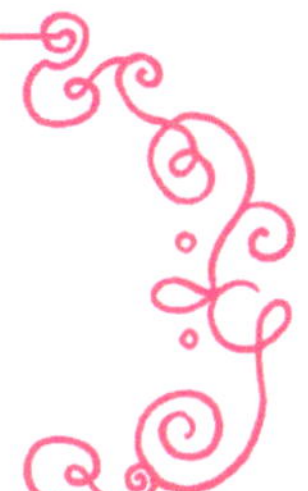

CRÈME BRÛLÉE

Fun With A Torch • Serves 4-5 • **GF, V**

½ Cup of Sugar, Divided • 1 ¾ Cups of Heavy Cream
4 Egg Yolks • Pinch of Salt • 1 Teaspoon Vanilla Extract
¼ Cup of Brown Sugar

- Pre-heat oven to 325 °. Boil a kettle of water.

- In a medium saucepan, combine ¼ cup of the sugar and the cream over medium-low heat and stir gently until the mixture warms, about 6-8 minutes. Do not let the mixture boil.

- In a separate bowl, whisk the remaining ¼ cup sugar, the egg yolks, and salt until very creamy, about 3-4 minutes by hand.

- Slowly and gradually whisk the warm cream mixture into the egg mixture. This is called tempering and will keep the eggs from scrambling.

- Put a mesh strainer over a large bowl and strain mixture to catch any little bits of egg. Stir in the vanilla extract. You now have a custard mixture!

- Place four or five 6-ounce ramekins on a baking sheet and use a ladle to fill the ramekins almost all the way to the top with your custard mixture.

- Place the baking sheet in the oven. Very carefully fill the baking sheet with boiling water from the kettle until the depth of the water is half the depth of the ramekins. Take care not to get any water in the custard, or it may not set properly.

- Bake for 30-40 minutes until the custard is barely set in the center. Test with a clean knife, which should come out with just a little custard on the tip. You want it to be ever so slightly undercooked! Carefully remove ramekins from baking pan with a spatula and let cool to room temperature, then refrigerate for at least 4 hours.

- Distribute a few large pinches of brown sugar thinly and evenly over the top of each custard. Carefully use a kitchen torch to caramelize the sugar until it forms a hard, brittle crust. Serve immediately!

NOTA BENE: Shallower ramekins have more surface area for the crunchy burnt sugar, whereas the taller types allow the creaminess of the custard to be emphasized. In any case, the custard cooks at about the same rate in both types.

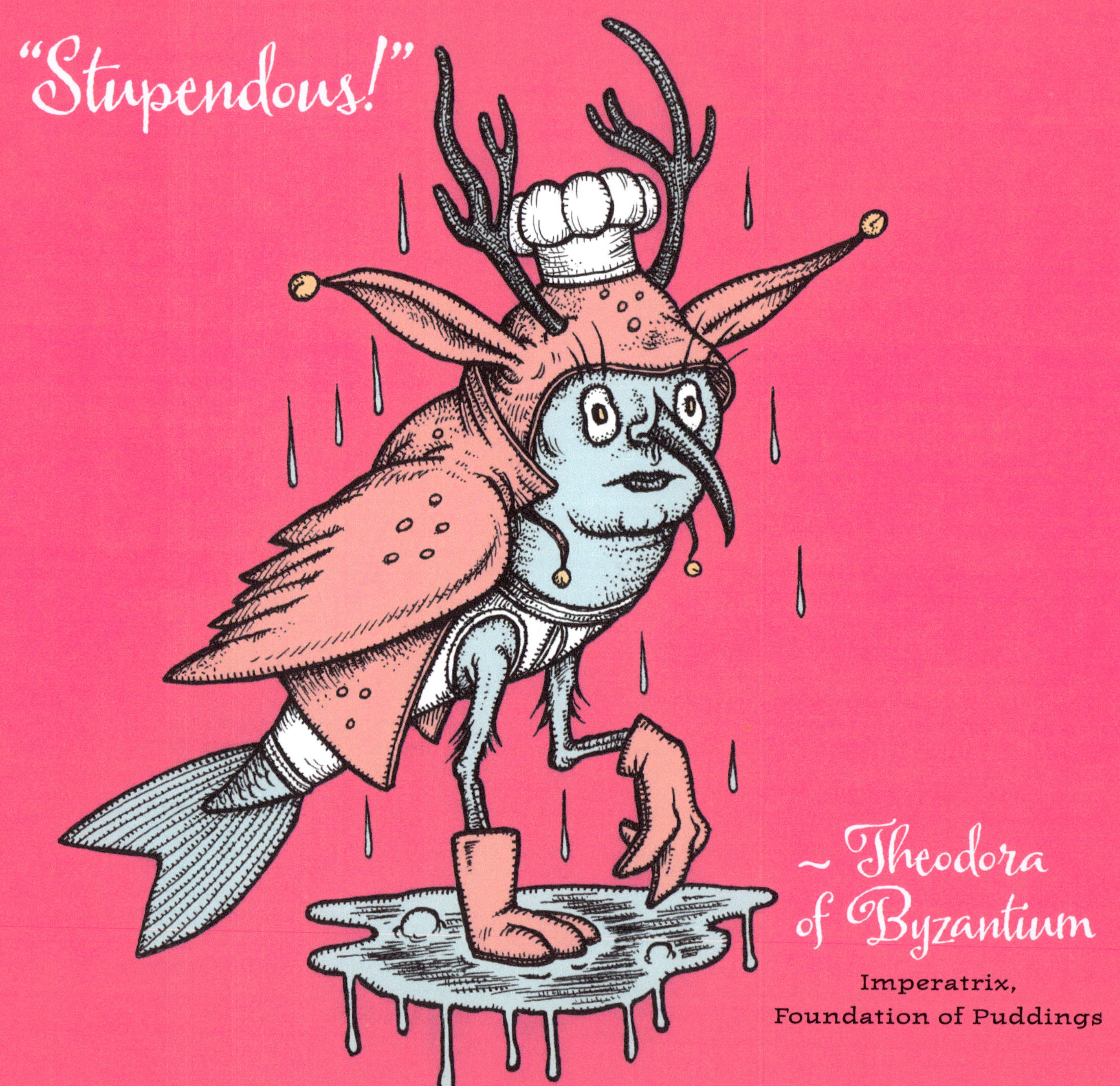

"Stupendous!"
~ Theodora of Byzantium
Imperatrix,
Foundation of Puddings

CHOCOLATE BREAD PUDDING

I Will Go Whither I Must To Get What Pudding I May • Serves 9 • **V**

1 Stick of Butter • 5 Cups of Nice Artisan Bread
1 ½ Cups of Heavy Cream • 1 ½ Cups of Milk
10 Oz. Bittersweet Chocolate Chips Containing 50-70% Cocoa Solids
6 Egg Yolks • 1 Cup of Sugar • ½ Teaspoon Vanilla Extract • More Butter

- Gently melt butter in a microwave or on the stove top.

- Cut the crusts off your bread, then cut the bread into one-inch cubes –or–tear it if you want a rustic pudding. Don't use supermarket-style sandwich bread, get artisan baguettes or loaves from a bakery. You can also make your own bread, see Interesting Resources on Page 71!

- Place the bread in a large bowl and pour the melted butter over it. Combine thoroughly. Eat one!

- In a medium saucepan, heat the cream and milk over medium-low heat and slowly add the chocolate until it's incorporated. Do not let the mixture boil. If the chocolate seems grainy, don't worry.

- In a separate bowl, whisk the egg yolks together and then whisk in the sugar.

- Slowly and gradually whisk the warm chocolate cream mixture into the egg mixture. This is called tempering and will keep the eggs from scrambling. Scrape any remaining bits of chocolate from the pan into the mixture. Add vanilla extract and stir to combine. You now have a custard mixture!

- Pour the chocolate custard mixture over bread. Let stand for an hour or two at room temperature, allowing the bread to absorb the chocolate flavor.

- Pre-heat oven to 350 °.

- Butter a 9" flameproof baking dish and carefully add the chocolaty bread mixture. The bread will have expanded while soaking, so if you have too much, don't overfill the baking dish! Place baking dish on a baking sheet to catch any liquid spills and then place in the oven.

- Bake 35-45 minutes, until the custard has set around the edges. Let cool for 1 hour so it sets completely, then serve re-warmed with vanilla ice cream or whipped cream!

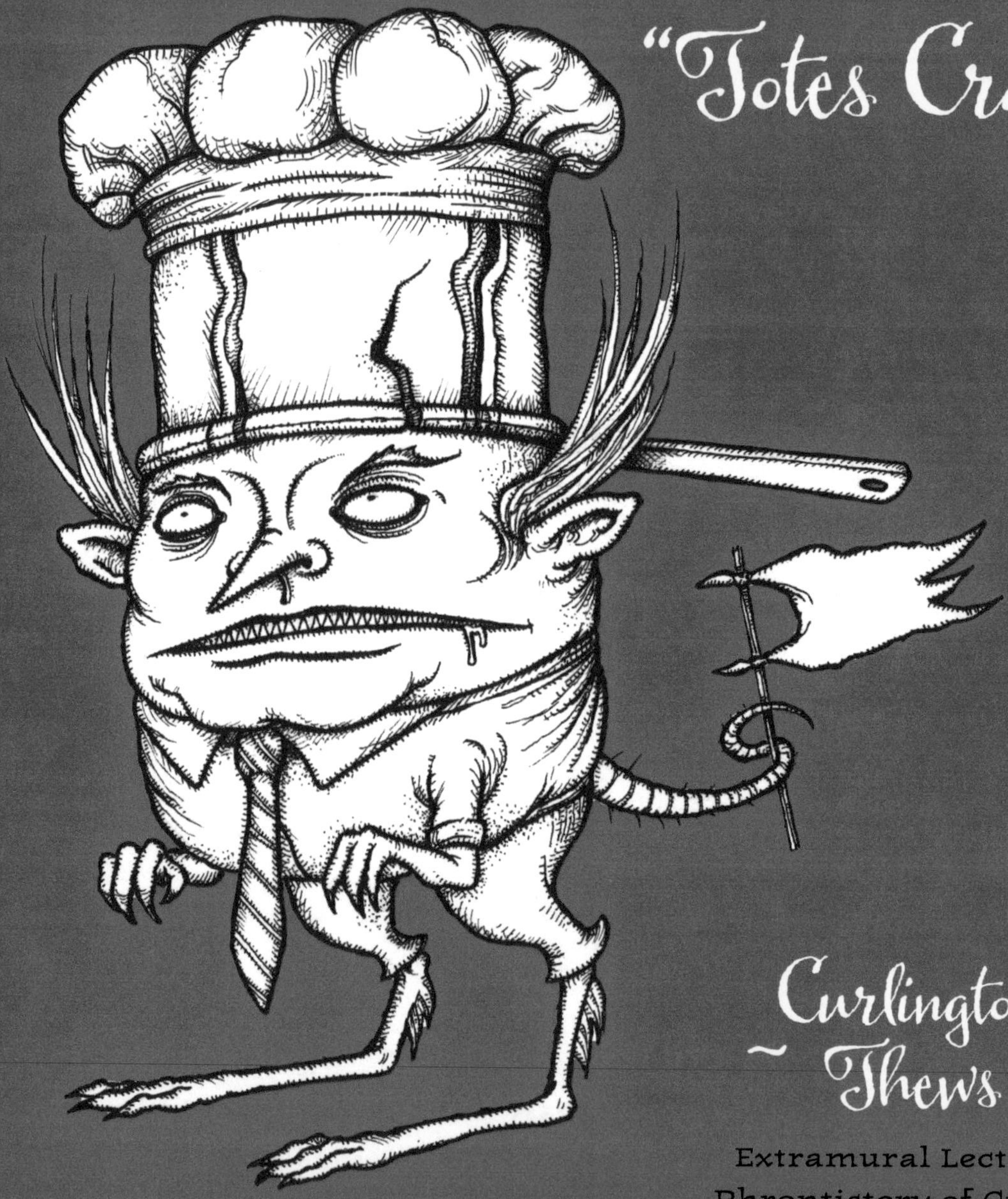

"Totes Cray!"
Curlington
~ Thews
Extramural Lecturer,
Phrontistery of Creams

PISTACHIO ICE CREAM

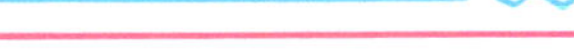

Christmas On A Spoon • Serves 6-8 • **GF, V**

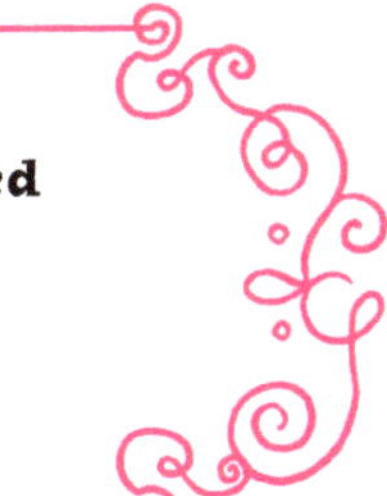

¾ Cup of Sugar • Pinch of Salt • 2 Cups of Heavy Cream, Divided
1 Cup of Whole Milk • 1 Whole Vanilla Bean
2 ¼ Cups of Shelled Unsalted Pistachios, Divided
6 Egg Yolks • ½ Teaspoon Almond Extract

- In a medium saucepan, combine the sugar, salt, one cup of cream, the milk, and the vanilla bean and cook over medium-low heat. Stir gently until the mixture warms, about 8 minutes. Do not let the mixture boil.

- Remove cream mixture from heat. Add two cups of pistachios to the mixture, cover and let steep at room temperature for one or two hours.

- Remove the vanilla bean. Use a mesh strainer to strain the pistachio-infused cream mixture into a separate saucepan, pressing down to extract as much flavor as possible from the nuts. Pulse two tablespoons of the spent pistachios in a food processor and discard the rest.

- In another bowl, whisk the egg yolks until lightly beaten.

- Re-warm the pistachio cream mixture. Taste it!

- Slowly and gradually whisk the warm pistachio cream mixture into the eggs. This is called tempering and will keep the eggs from scrambling. Cook the egg and cream mixture over medium heat, stirring until it is thick enough to coat the back of a spatula. You'll know.

- In yet another bowl, add the remaining 1 cup of cream. Put a mesh strainer over the bowl and strain the egg and cream mixture to catch any little bits of cooked egg. Remove the strainer and add in the pulsed pistachios from Step 3. Add almond extract and stir to combine. You now have a custard mixture! Chill covered in the refrigerator until very cold.

- Pour the custard into your ice cream maker, following the manufacturer's instructions. You can get a remarkably good machine online for about $40. Just before the ice cream is done, slowly add the remaining ¼ cup of fresh pistachios. Store in airtight containers and freeze for as long as you can wait, or overnight.

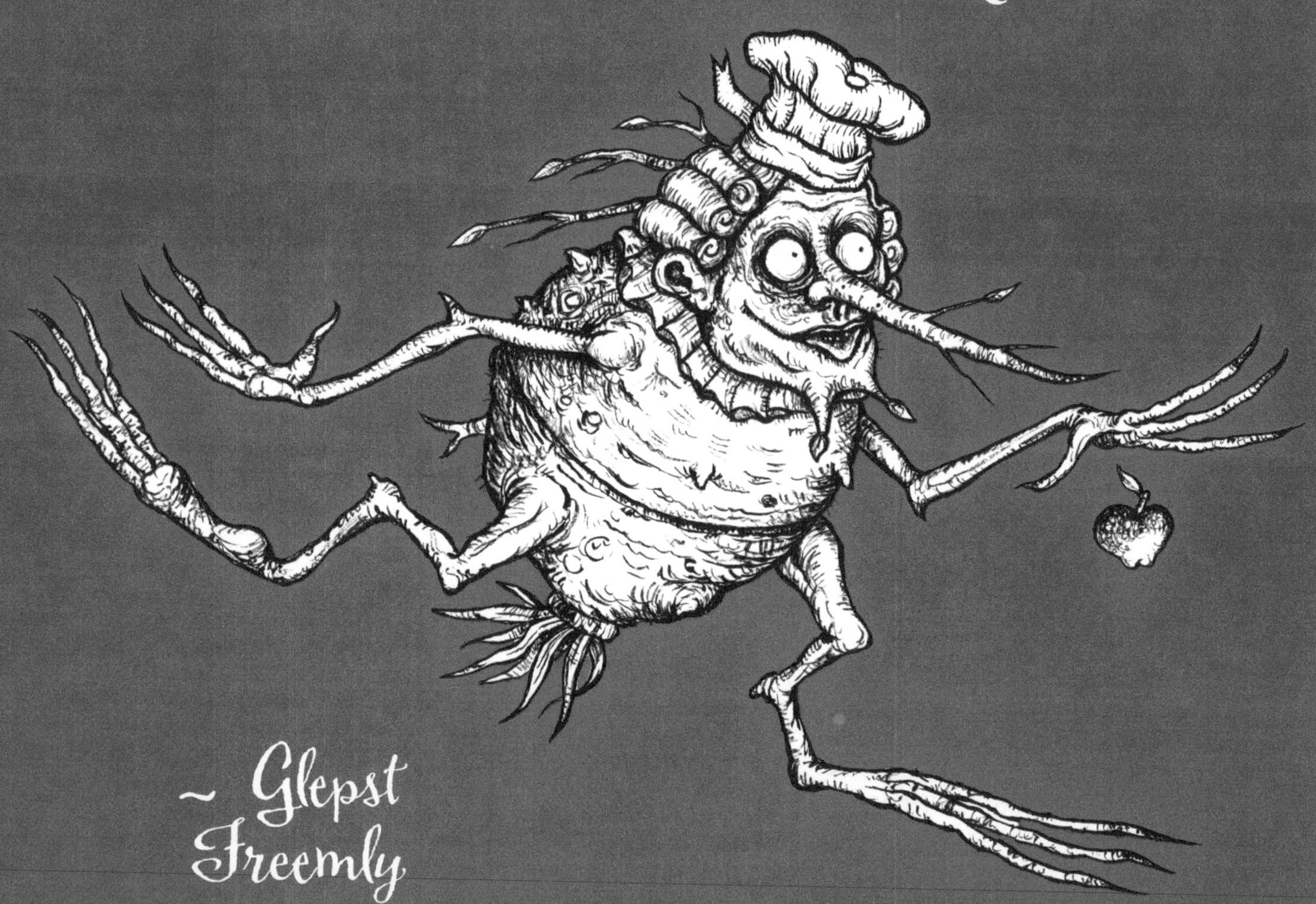
"Radical!"
~ Glepst Freemly
Head of Delicious Bibb,
College of Crisssp & Crunnnnchy

APPLE PIE

Piece of Cake! • Serves 8 • V

FOR THE DOUGH
10 Tablespoons of Cold Butter • 1 ¾ Cups of Flour • ¼ Cup of Sugar
Small Pinch of Salt • ⅓ Cup of Ice Water

FOR THE FILLING
8 Medium-Sized Granny Smith Apples • ¾ Cup of Sugar • 1 Tablespoon Lemon Juice
6 Tablespoons Butter • 2 Tablespoons Flour • 1 Tablespoon Ground Cinnamon • Pinch of Salt

FOR THE PIE
More Butter • 1 Egg • 2 or 3 Generous Pinches of Sugar

- Cut cold butter into small cubes – the smaller, the better!

- Add the flour, sugar and salt to a large bowl and mix together. Add the butter cubes and combine with flour mixture using a pastry blender. Blend until the flour and butter mixture is combined, about 8 minutes. The result should be a fragrant, grainy mixture, almost like small couscous. Almost.

- Alternatively, you can do the step above in a food processor. Time is cut in half, but the result should be the same fragrant, grainy mixture.

- Slowly incorporate the ice water until the dough is combined. It should be only slightly tacky. Add more ice water or flour if needed to get the right texture. Divide in half, press between pieces of wax paper and refrigerate for at least two hours.

- Peel, core and slice the apples. In a pre-heated sautée pan, cook the apples over medium heat with the sugar, lemon juice and butter, about 3-4 minutes. Add the flour, cinnamon and salt and cook until the juices start to thicken a bit, about 2 minutes. Taste and add a little sugar if needed. Let cool to room temperature.

- Roll out the pie dough on a floured surface with a floured rolling pin. Create two roughly similar disks of dough that will fit your pie plate.

- Pre-heat your oven to 375 °. Butter your pie plate. Add one disk of dough to the bottom of the plate, stretching as needed to fit. Patch little holes with extra dough. Re-roll if there are big holes. Fill with the cooled pie filling. Dot with butter.

- Place the second dough disk over filled pie. Crimp edges with a fork, and cut away any extra dough. Cut several vents in the top of the pie with a sharp knife.

- Beat an egg in a small bowl. Glaze the pie with the beaten egg using a basting brush. Generously sprinkle sugar over the magnificently glistening egg.

- Place the pie plate on a baking sheet to catch any liquid spills and then place in oven. Bake about 45 minutes, until the crust is golden-brown. Let cool and serve warm with ice cream!

NOTA BENE: If you want to slice the apples a little ahead of time, you can place them in a bowl of acidulated water, see Page 31.

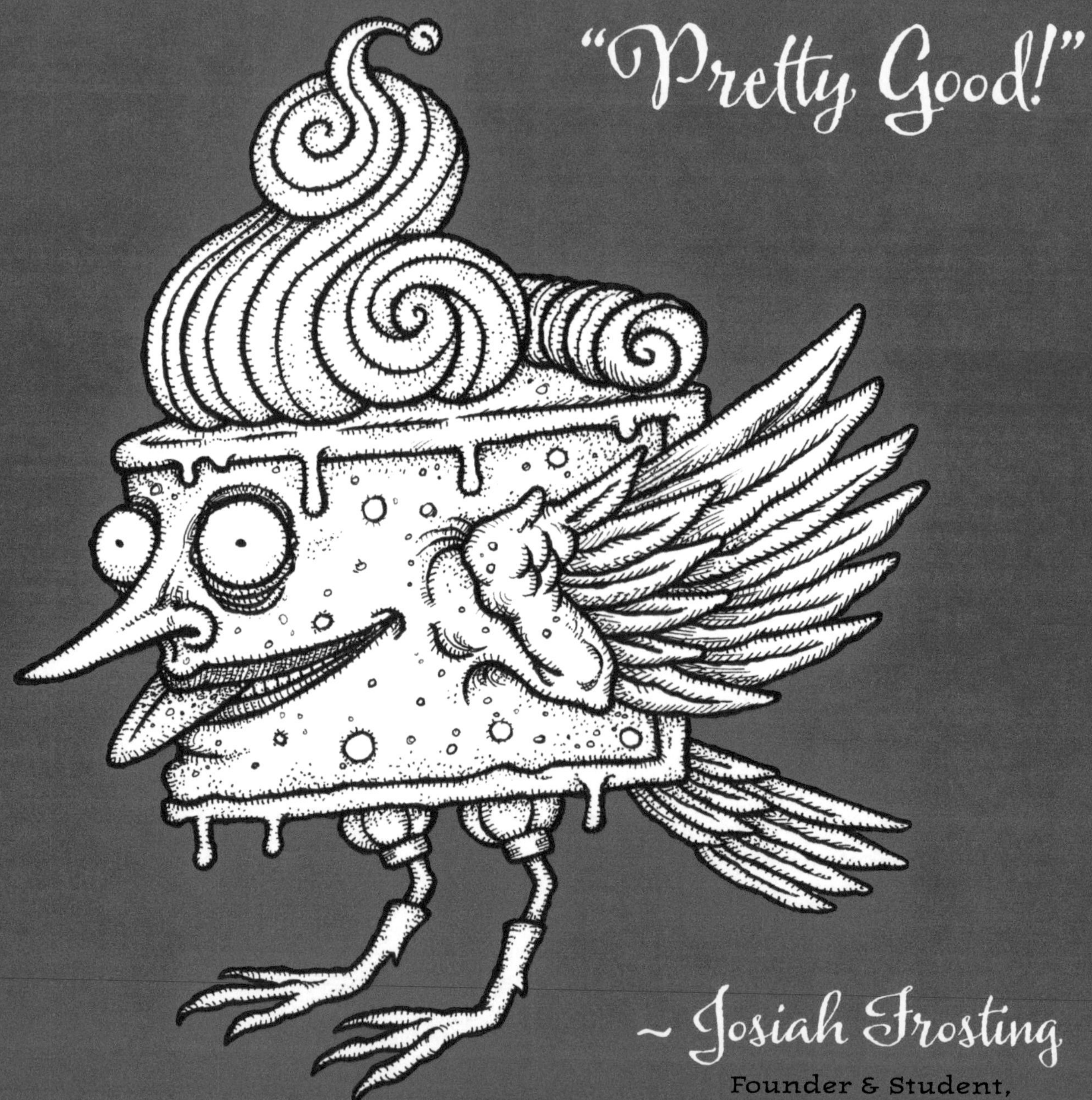

"Pretty Good!"
~ Josiah Frosting
Founder & Student,
Frosting University

FROSTING'S CUPPYCAKES

Make Your Dentist Rich! • Serves 12 • V

FOR THE CUPPYCAKES

1 ½ Cups of Flour • 1 Teaspoon Baking Powder • ½ Cup of Softened Butter
1 Cup of Sugar • 2 Eggs • 2 Teaspoons Vanilla Extract • ⅔ Cup of Milk • Pink Food Coloring

FOR THE FROSTING

2 Cups of Confectioner's Sugar • ⅔ Cup of Softened Butter • 1 Teaspoon Vanilla Extract
A Little Heavy Cream –or– Milk • Blue Food Coloring
Your Choice of Cuppycake Decorations

- Pre-heat oven to 350 °.

- Combine the flour and baking powder in a large bowl.

- In another large bowl, use a hand-held mixer to beat the butter until smooth –or– use a stand mixer. Add the sugar and beat at medium-high speed until creamy, 3-4 minutes.

- Lower the mixer speed and add the eggs, milk, vanilla extract and pink food coloring. Mix for 2-3 minutes to combine.

- Slowly add the flour mixture until combined. Add more food coloring if needed, mixing to combine. You now have delicious cuppycake batter!

- Line a muffin tin with colorful paper cuppycake liners. Use a spatula to fill the liners with batter, just below the top of the pan. Bake for about 20 minutes, until a knife comes out clean. Let cool.

- In another large bowl, combine the confectioner's sugar and butter at medium speed with a hand-held mixer –or– use a stand mixer. Add the vanilla, cream –or– milk and blue food coloring and beat at a higher speed until the texture is just right for spreading on cuppycakes. You'll know.

- Frost cuppycakes with a pastry –or– butter knife. For even fancier cuppycakes, pipe the frosting through a decorative nozzle with a pastry bag. Pile it high! Decorate as needed. Ho-ho!

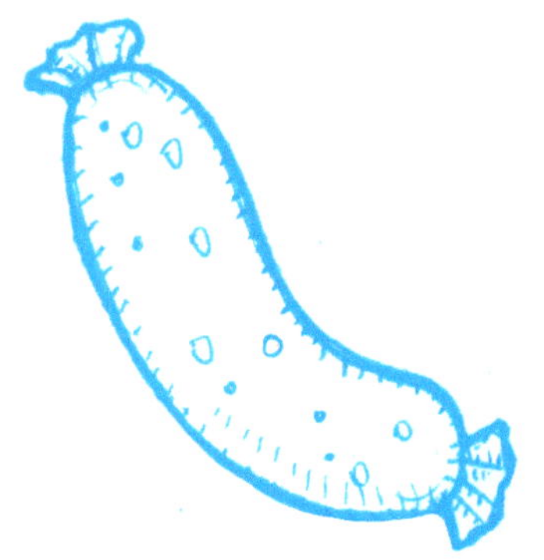

SELECTED

LAZY MEALS

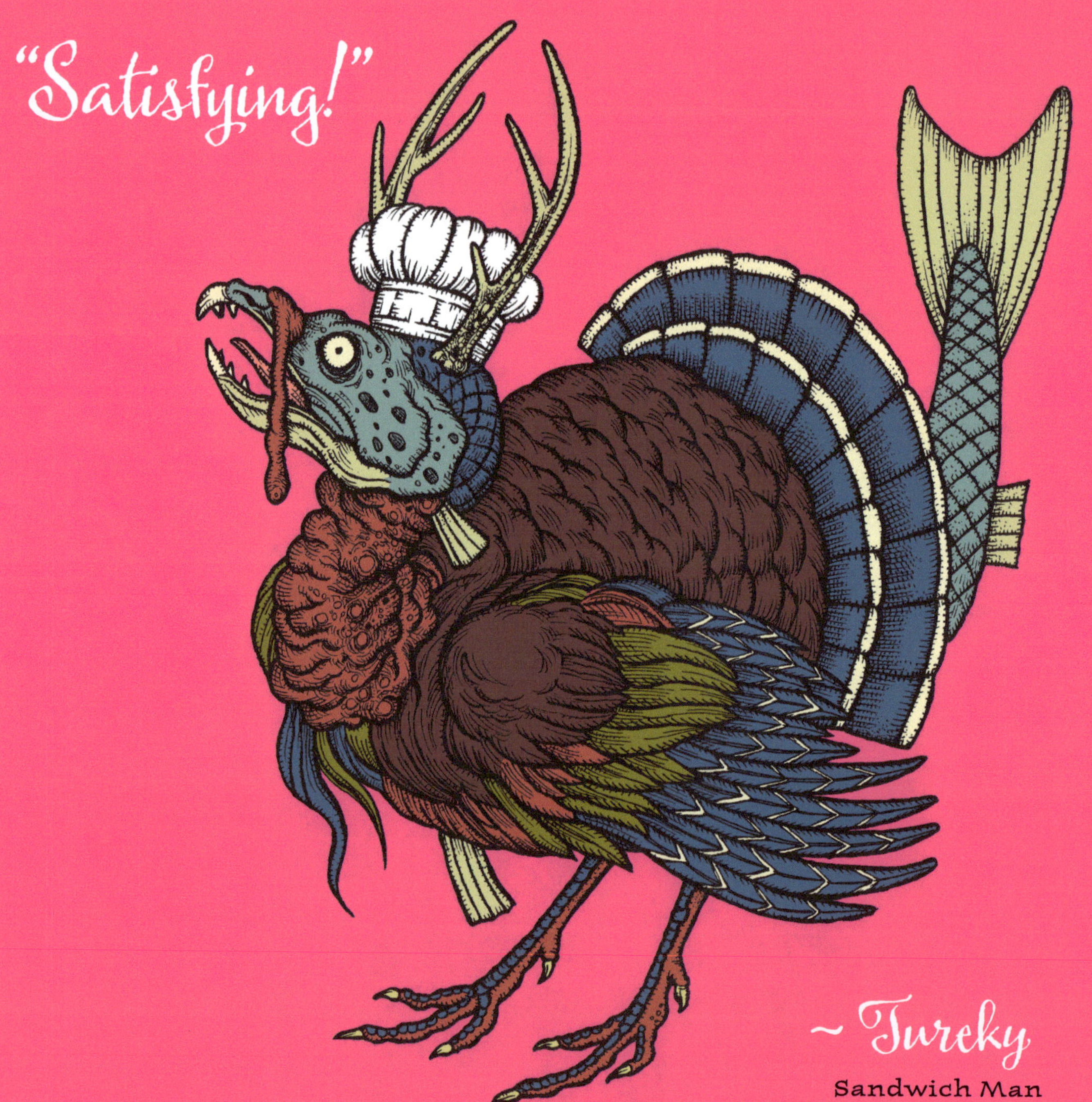

"Satisfying!"
~ Tureky
Sandwich Man

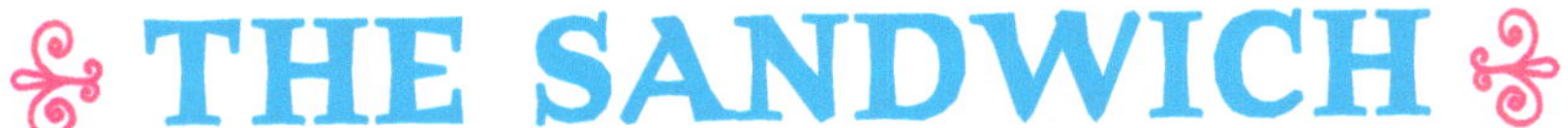

THE SANDWICH

Don't Scoff • Serves 1 • Can Be **GF, V, VG**

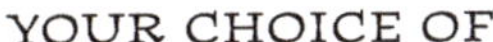

YOUR CHOICE OF

Meats • Cheeses • Vegetables • Breads • Condiments • Chips

- Go to a grocery store that sells nice things and treat yourself to anything that would make an interesting sandwich.

- Consider the meats and cheeses in the deli case. Don't know what something is? Get some! There's only one way to find out what Havarti or mortadella might be.

- Peruse the produce section for interesting onions and exotic lettuces. Some people even like raw tomatoes and avocados on their sandwiches, can you imagine that?

- The baked goods section likely has breadstuffs with which you are not familiar. Get some Dutch crunch rolls or pita bread!

- The condiments section will have a great host of unusual pickles and surprising mustards.

- Don't forget the chips! You can't have a sandwich without chips. That bag of Sriracha and bleu cheese crisps is calling your name.

- Bring it all home, arrange as necessary on your bread, apply condiments with glee, pile some chips on your plate, open a beer and feel good about saving money on your utility bills!

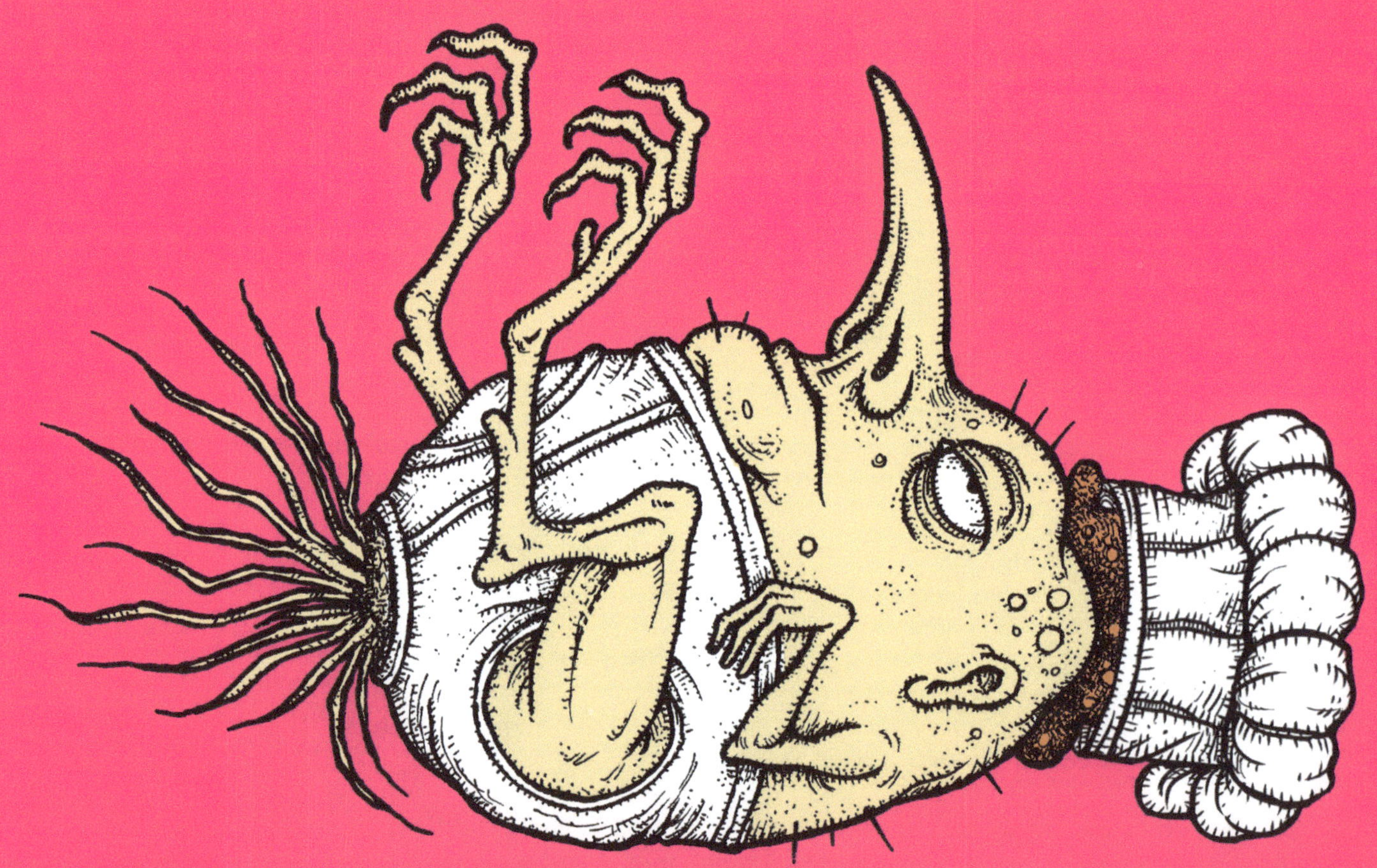

"Super Exciting."

~ Dinkus
Podames

Director of Enthusiasm,
Hall of Cakes & Treats

SPAGHETTI alla PARMIGIANA

Forgot To Go Shopping? • Serves 2 • V

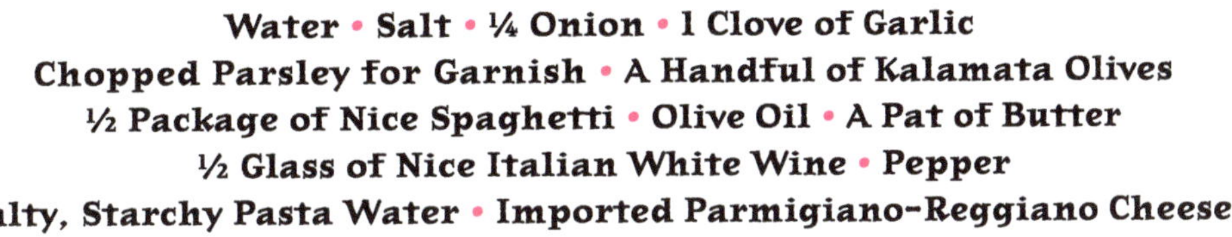

Water • Salt • ¼ Onion • 1 Clove of Garlic
Chopped Parsley for Garnish • A Handful of Kalamata Olives
½ Package of Nice Spaghetti • Olive Oil • A Pat of Butter
½ Glass of Nice Italian White Wine • Pepper
Salty, Starchy Pasta Water • Imported Parmigiano-Reggiano Cheese

- In a medium to large saucepan, start boiling water for pasta. Salt it generously!

- Peel the onion and garlic. Finely chop the onion, garlic and parsley. Pit and slice Kalamata olives, if needed. Set aside onion and garlic in one small bowl, olives in another and parsley in a third.

- Cook the spaghetti per package directions, noting suggested cooking time.

- While the spaghetti is cooking, add a generous amount of olive oil to a gently pre-heated sautée pan. When oil is heated, add a pat of butter. Once the butter has melted, stir it into the olive oil using a wooden spatula.

- Cook the onion and garlic in the oil and butter until soft, about 3-4 minutes. Add the wine and bring to boil to cook out the alcohol, about 1 minute, then cook over medium-high heat to reduce liquid by half. Season with salt and pepper.

- Your spaghetti should be nearly cooked by now. When it is almost al dente, use tongs to transfer the spaghetti into the sautée pan. Add a bit of the salty, starchy pasta water and cook at medium-high heat for 1 minute.

- Remove from heat. Add in the olives. Grate in a generous amount of Parmigiano-Reggiano cheese (accept no substitute!) and crack some pepper into the pasta. Stir to combine.

- Taste it – it probably needs lots more cheese. Adjust other seasonings as needed.

- Add the spaghetti to pasta bowls, garnish with parsley and serve with even more cheese, a glass of the nice Italian white wine and a lovely green salad. Mangia tutti!

NOTA BENE: This dish lends itself to lots of variations. Consider using red bell peppers, sun-dried tomatoes, leftover chicken, or whatever else you have in your fridge or pantry!

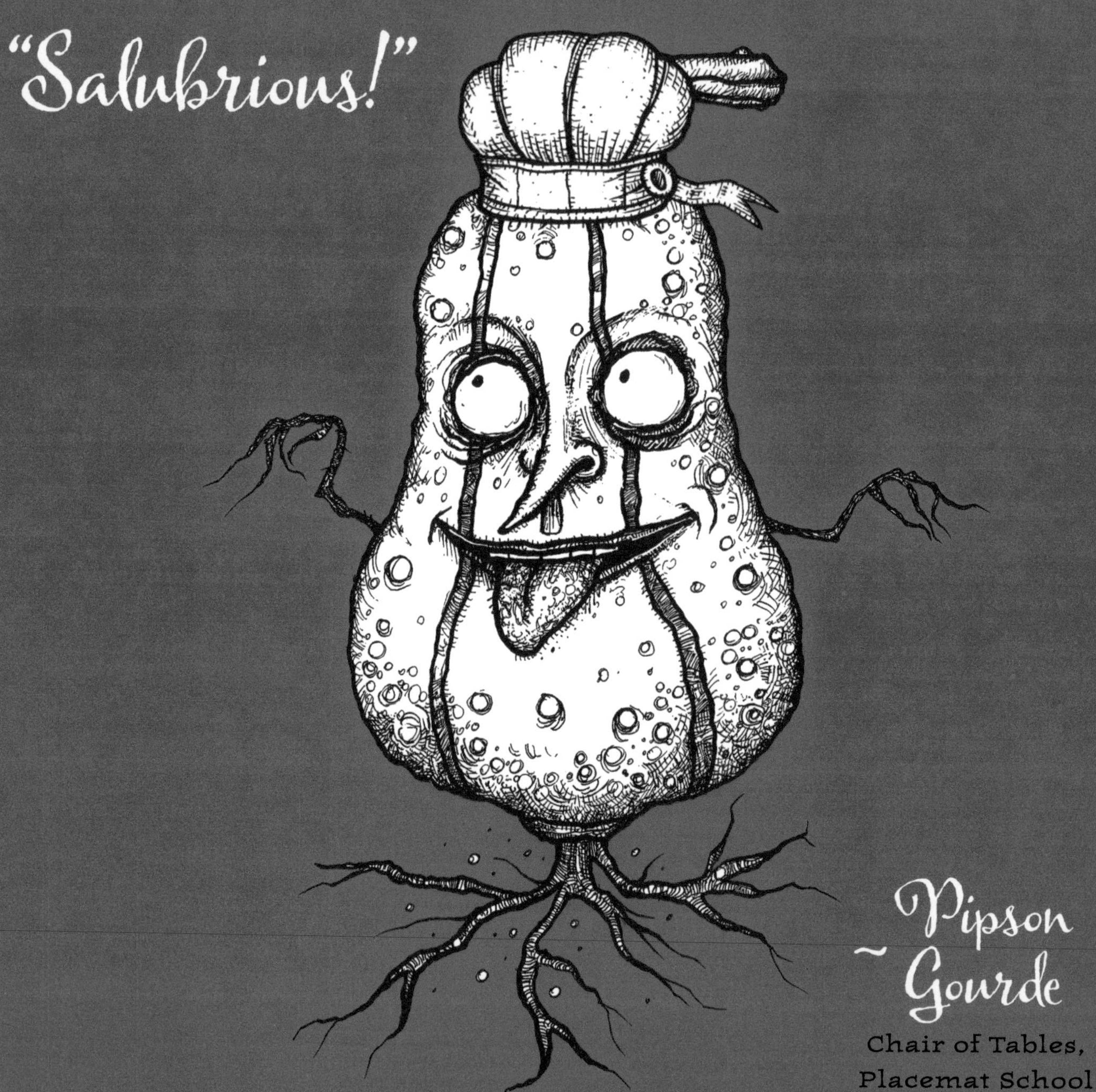

"Salubrious!"

~ Pipson
Gourde
Chair of Tables,
Placemat School

CHICKEN SALAD *with* SOY DRESSING

Quick and Satisfying • Serves 2 • **GF**

FOR THE DRESSING
2 Tablespoons Soy Sauce • 2 ½ Tablespoons Rice Wine Vinegar • Dash of Sesame Oil
2 Tablespoons Avocado Oil • 2 Tablespoons Honey • ½ Tablespoon Dijon Mustard
FOR THE SALAD
¼ Head of Cabbage • ¼ Head of Bibb Lettuce • ⅓ Red Bell Pepper
⅓ Green Bell Pepper • 2 Scallions • ⅓ Cup Cashews • 1 Boneless Skinless Chicken Breast
Salt • Pepper • Avocado Oil • 1 Tablespoon Sesame Seeds for Garnish

- Create a salad dressing by whisking the soy sauce, rice wine vinegar, sesame oil, honey and mustard in a small bowl until lightly emulsified. Adjust flavor as desired. Pour into cruet and set aside.

- Finely shred cabbage with a long, sharp knife. Chop or slice the lettuce, and thinly slice the red and green peppers. Trim the root ends of the scallions and then slice them diagonally (a.k.a "on the bias"). Place all of the vegetables in a large mixing bowl and toss to combine.

- Gently crush the cashews with the flat of your knife. Add these to the rest of your salad, tossing to combine.

- Place your chicken breast on a cutting board, place plastic wrap over it, and pound it thinner with the flat part of a meat mallet. Remove the plastic, dry your chicken with paper towels and season it on both sides with salt and pepper. Wash your hands.

- In a gently pre-heated large sautée pan, add a medium amount of avocado oil. When oil is heated, transfer your chicken to the pan. Sautée the chicken over medium heat, flipping once, until the temperature reaches 165° –or– the juices run clear, about 8-10 minutes.

- Let your chicken rest on a clean cutting board for 5-10 minutes, then slice into strips.

- Divide your salad mixture into two large bowls. Place chicken over salads, then sprinkle sesame seeds over the top of each. Give dressing a quick shake in the cruet and serve!

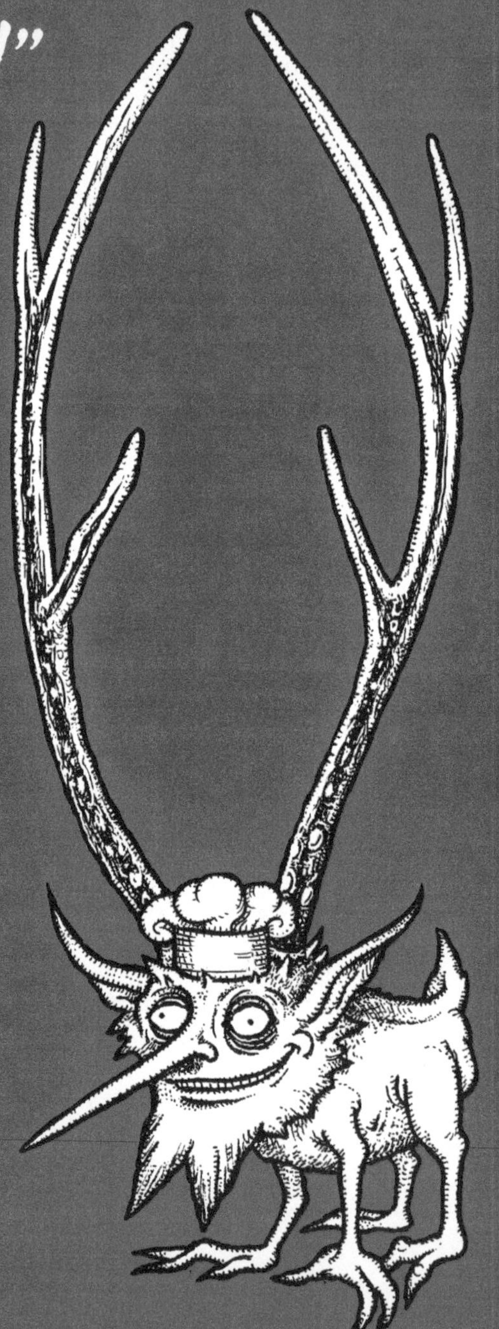

"Fantastico!"
~ Chuckie Pivens
Brigadier, Chiffonades and Aromatics

BASIL PESTO

Thus It Was in the Days of Basilicus • Serves 4–6 • **GF, V**

1 Bunch of Fresh Basil • 2 or 3 Cloves of Garlic
Salt • Pepper • Imported Parmigiano-Reggiano Cheese
1 Cup of Walnuts –or– Pine Nuts • Olive Oil

- Wash basil well, removing any unsightly bits. Dry thoroughly.

- Place basil in a food processor with the garlic, a bit of salt and pepper, a rather generous amount of grated Parmigiano-Reggiano cheese, and the walnuts –or– pine nuts. Pulse a few times to combine.

- Switch on food processor and slowly introduce olive oil until the mixture is paste-like. It shouldn't be too runny or oily. Scrape sides with a spatula as needed.

- Taste and adjust seasoning. You should almost always add more cheese.

- Serve over cooked linguine –or– gnocchi. Alternatively, make a cold pasta salad with kalamata olives and grape tomatoes! Pesto is also great as a spread on turkey sandwiches.

- Any leftover pesto should be placed in an airtight container with a thin layer of olive oil over it to keep it from browning. It'll last in the fridge for a few days. When ready to use, mix thoroughly.

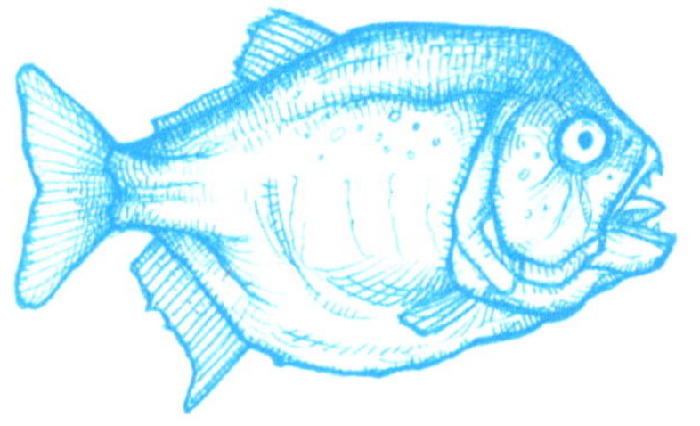

PLEASE

DO NOT ATTEMPT

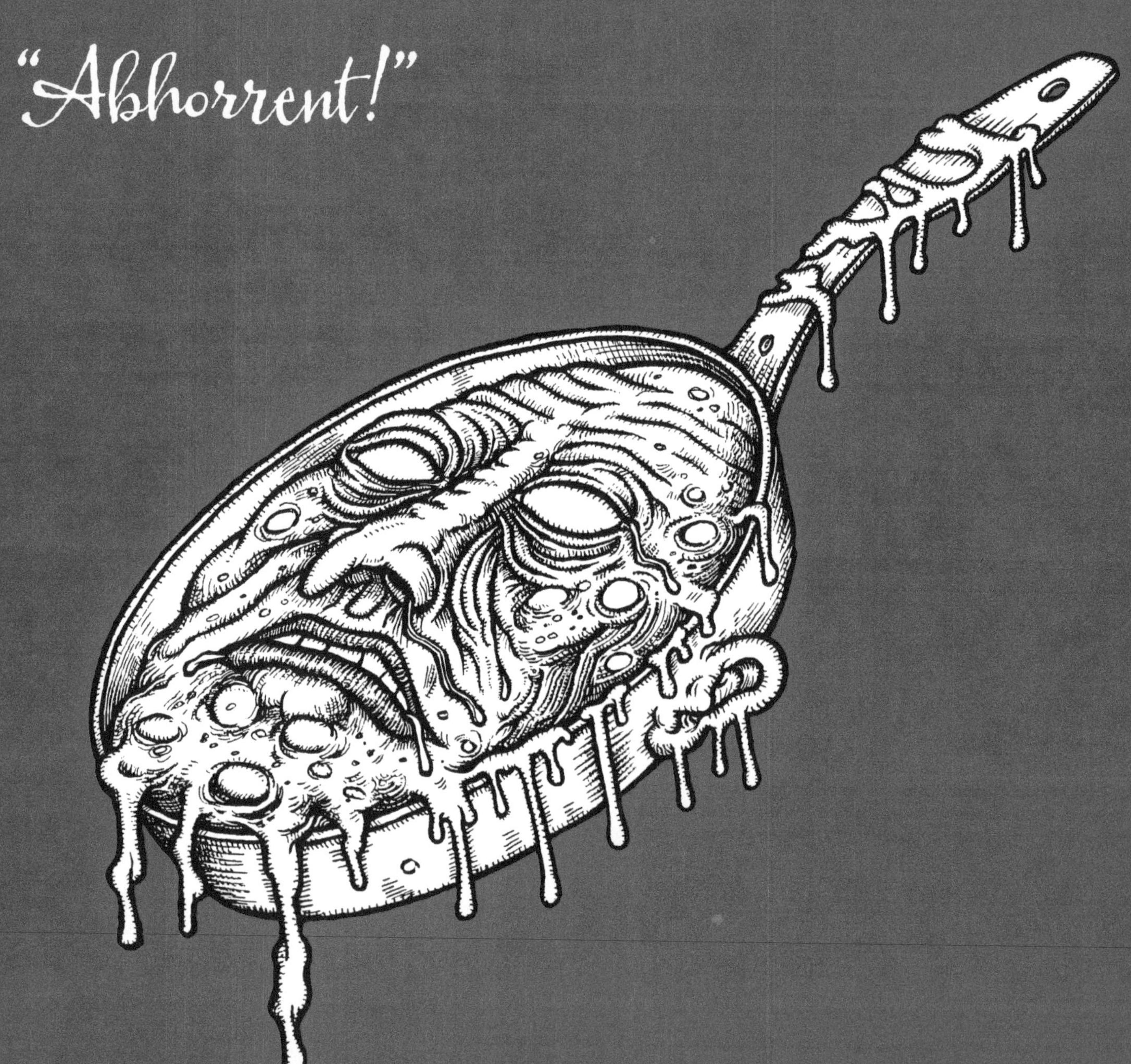
"Abhorrent!"

❦ HEAVY BALCH ❦

Ruin Your Pan! • Serves 1 Executive • V

A Goodly Amount of Treacle • A Slathering of Molasses
A Smidge of Simple Syrup • 1 Bottle of Pure Vermont Maple Syrup
A Ramekin of Lavender Honey • 1 Jar of Apricot Jam
2 Onions • Olio Lampante • 1 Pound of Rye Flour
1 Liter of Sarsaparilla To Taste

- In a very large sautée pan, cook the treacle, molasses, syrups, honey and jam on very high heat until a most putrid smoke is evident. Remove from heat.

- Roughly chop the onions. Heat a second sautée pan and add a splash of olio lampante. Cook onions until deep brown, stirring infrequently, about 45 minutes. Remove from heat.

- Reheat the treacle syrup mixture until bubbling fiercely. Add the onions and the flour, and combine laboriously.

- Thin sauce with sarsaparilla until it is the consistency of molasses. Heat until boiling.

- Serve hot over Coq au Vin (see Nota Bene on Page 15) or locally sourced cucumbers.

WARNING: This piquant dish is for members of the Executive Class only. All others will be brusquely rebuffed!

FOR NECROMANCERS: Heavy Balch may be used as a foundation for the creation of many noxious salves, foul elixirs, noisome potions, foetid remedies and mephitic unguents.

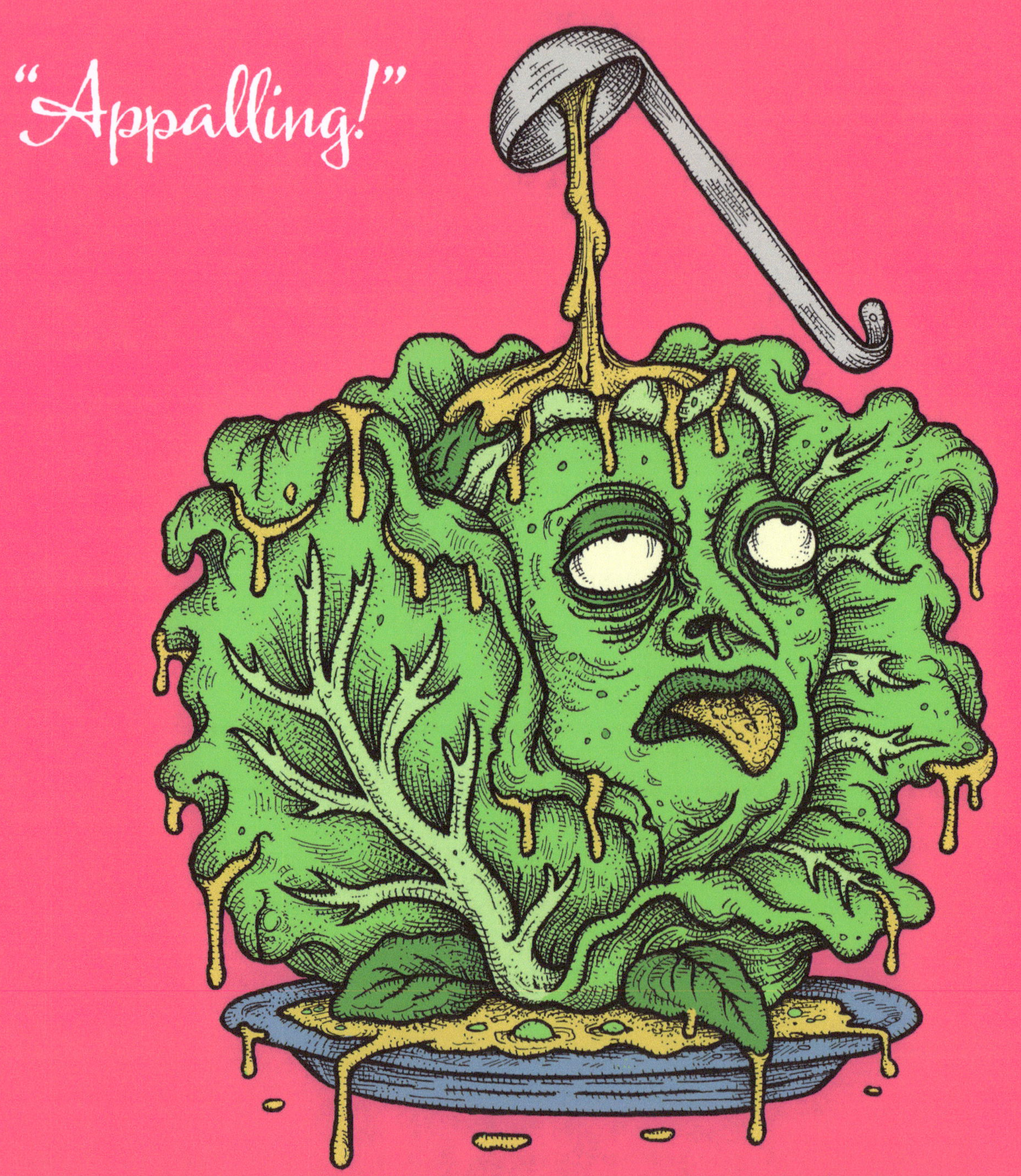

"Appalling!"

CABBAGE *with* STIFLING GRAVIES

Être Dans Les Choux • Serves 12 (Great For Parties)

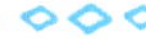

FOR THE FIRST GRAVY
1 Cup of Margarine • 1 Cup of All-Purpose Flour • 2 Cups of Orange Juice
FOR THE SECOND GRAVY
1 Cup of Lard • 1 Cup of Wheat Flour • 2 Cups of Pickle Juice
FOR THE FINAL DISH
1 Head of Cabbage • Artificial Bacon Bits • Sour Cream
Parsley for Garnish

- **In a medium saucepan, create a roux by combining the margarine and flour. Stir constantly until it is golden brown, about 10-12 minutes.**

- **Add the orange juice slowly, whisking to combine. Cook until it is a thick, rich gravy, about 15 minutes. Set aside.**

THE FIRST ESCULENT GRAVY IS ENQUICKENED, CLAP NOW THINE EYES UPON IT!

- **In another medium saucepan, create a roux by combining the lard and flour. Stir constantly until it is golden brown, about 10-12 minutes.**

- **Add the pickle juice slowly, whisking to combine. Cook until it is a thick, rich gravy, about 15 minutes. Set aside.**

WHOMSOEVER HAVETH EARS, LET THEM HARK UNTO THE SECOND PIQUANT GRAVY!

- **Re-heat both gravies until rather hot.**

- **Place the cabbage on a large serving plate. Generously ladle the first gravy over the cabbage. Then carefully ladle the second gravy over the first gravy.**

- **Generously sprinkle the bacon bits over the gravied cabbage, and place a dollop of sour cream at the very top of the cabbage. Garnish with parsley and serve forth.**

REGARD NOW THE CABBAGE, ENSTIFLED! ART THOU NOT PLEASED?

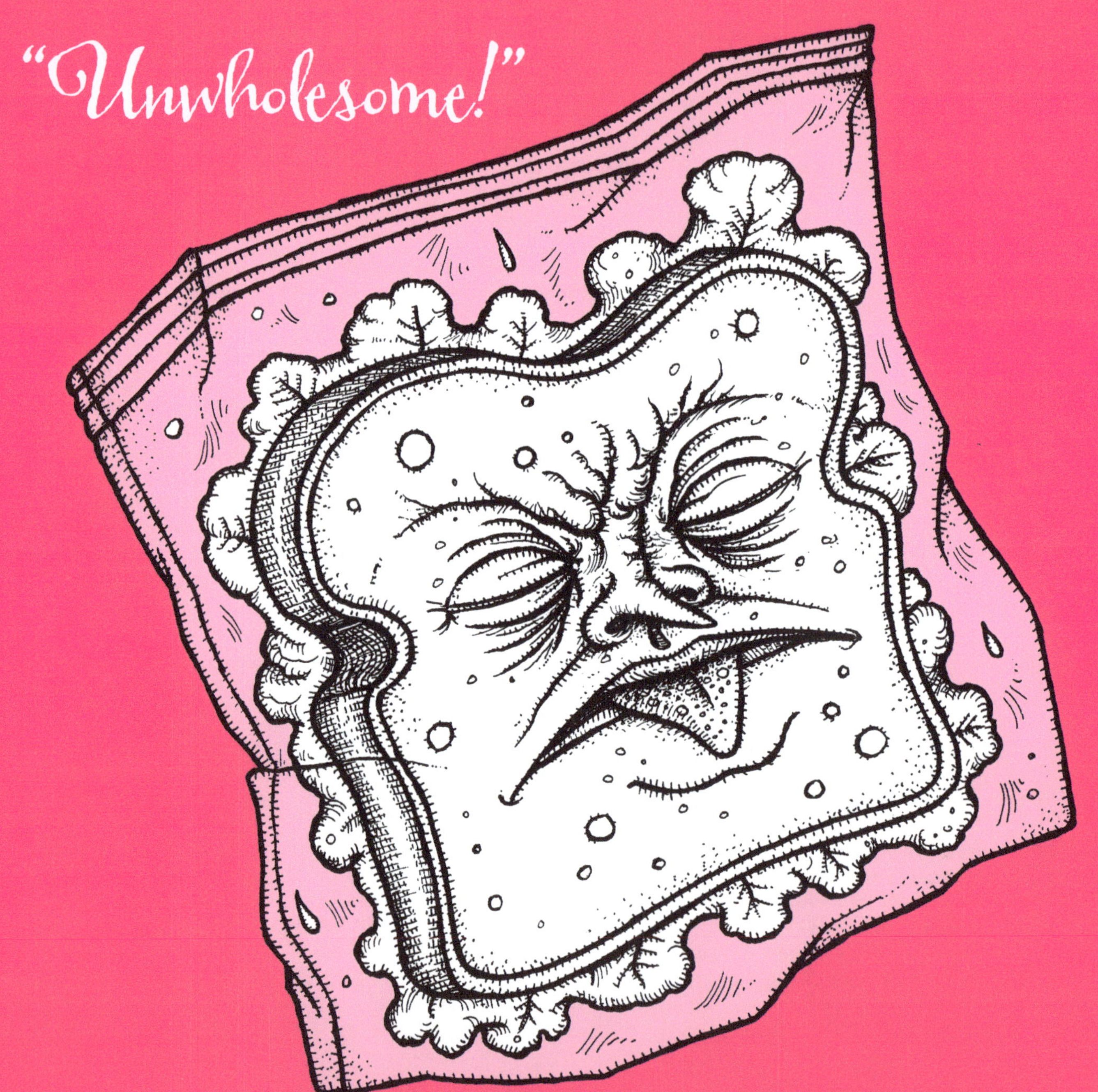

"Unwholesome!"

THE HOMUNCULUS

Intro to Alchemy • Serves No-One • Can Be **GF, V, VG**

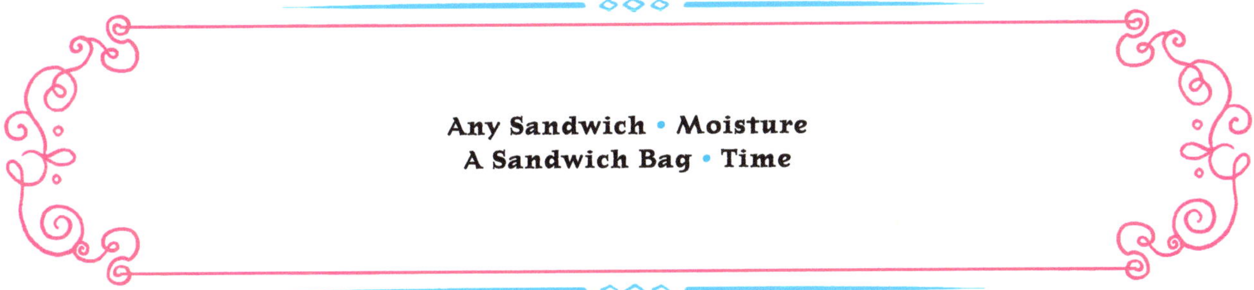

Any Sandwich • Moisture
A Sandwich Bag • Time

- Choose your sandwich with great judgement according to the principles delineated on Page 49 of this book.

- Admire your sandwich.

- Moisten the inside of a sandwich bag as you see fit. Gently place your sandwich in the bag and seal rather tightly.

- Carefully choose a location for your sandwich. This can be in a locker, at the back of the fridge, in the garage under some old boards, on the roof of your neighbor's house or in the glove compartment of your friend's car. Use your imagination!

- Place the sandwich at your chosen location precisely at midnight on the spring equinox.

- Forget your sandwich exists. Give it time. Go about your life. Get demoted. Cry in your milk. Rage impotently at the sun – all the usual things.

- During an episode of fitful sleep, remember the sandwich.

- Go to the location where you placed your sandwich and examine it.

- See if it has grown a face. If it has not, start over at Step One.

- If a small, semi-human face has sprouted, congratulations, you have taken the first step toward creating a homunculus!

AS ABOVE, SO BELOW

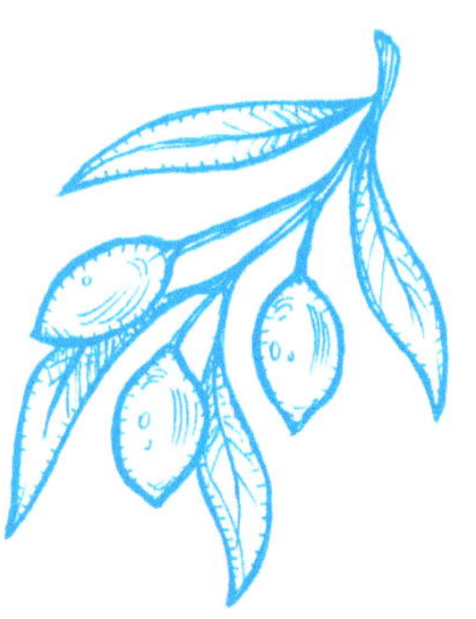

✤ ESSENTIAL PRINCIPLES ✤

USE THE FRESHEST & BEST INGREDIENTS YOU CAN GET.

Buy your meat from a reputable independent butcher or market.
Take advantage of farmers markets and buy local produce in season.
Be picky! Regard ordinary big-chain supermarkets with skepticism.

BUY QUALITY COOKWARE AND TAKE GOOD CARE OF IT.

Never invite disaster by leaving precious equipment strewn about the kitchen.
Always wash, dry and put away pans and knives immediately after using them.

DO IT CLEAN.

Work neatly, put your hair back, wear an apron, don't sneeze in the soup.
Always wash your hands before cooking and after touching raw meat, poultry and eggs.

SEASON YOUR FOOD.

Salt, pepper, herbs and spices are your friends.
Season a little at a time as you cook, layer your flavors and adjust at the end.
Think of time and temperature as ingredients.

COOK WITH ALL YOUR SENSES.

Smell your ingredients to determine freshness, **feel** how hot your pan is, **hear** how fast your onions are cooking, **see** that your meat is properly browned, and most importantly, always **taste** your food before you serve it.
Trust your intuition - if something doesn't seem right, it probably isn't.

PAY ATTENTION.

Put away your phone and turn off your TV so you can concentrate on cooking.
Take notes! Don't forget what you did and what you want to change next time.
Orient your attitude towards learning instead of performing.

EXPRESS YOURSELF.

Make every dish yours, you don't have to follow the recipe exactly. Experiment!

FOOD MADE WITH LOVE TASTES BETTER!

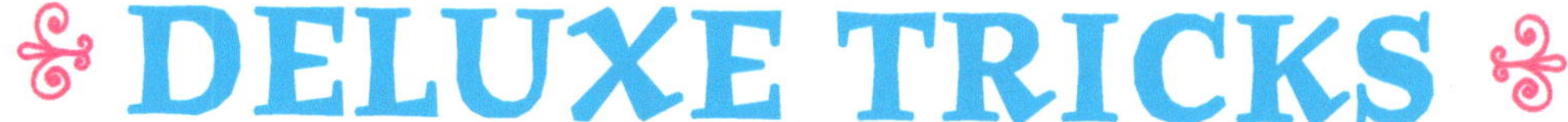

DELUXE TRICKS

EQUIPMENT

Two-cup deli containers (often free with takeout food!) are ideal for storage. Collect them and use a marker to write on the lids. They're perfect for fridge and freezer, they stack, have interchangeable lids, and are dishwasher-safe. Marvelous.

Keep your knives sharp!

Separate frozen hamburgers with an oyster shucker instead of a knife.

WINE

Cook with wine that's good enough to drink on its own.

Look for Italian wines that have the DOC or DOCG labels at the top of the neck. Similarly, look for French wines that say "AOC" on the label. They're usually great.

European wines typically give you more value for your money than American ones.

Avoid wines with cute names or funny labels, that's just marketing to sell plonk.

TECHNIQUES

When you fill a pot with water, get in the habit of always generously salting it.

Any pan is easier to clean while it's still hot - use scalding water and dish soap.

Memorize these temperatures: **125°** (Rare), **135°** (Medium-Rare), **145°** (Medium), **155°** (Medium-Well), **165°** (Well-Done -or- "Chicken is Cooked").

Plan your meals by utilizing all the ingredients you buy, don't waste anything!

Keep a well-stocked pantry (**Page 70**) for convenience and emergencies.

Start a freezer bag with chicken leftovers and bones and add to it as you accumulate scraps. You'll have enough for a soup stock (**Page 17**) before you know it.

Fresh herbs like parsley and cilantro will keep in the fridge for up to 2 weeks if you trim the stems and place them in a tall deli container with a little water at the bottom.

Cook in big batches and freeze the rest! For example, marinara sauce (**Page 27**) freezes wonderfully. Make it once and use it for 3 or 4 ready-to-defrost meals.

TOOLS OF THE TRADE

ESSENTIAL

One High-Quality Japanese Chef's Knife • Knife Sharpener
Deep Stainless Steel Mixing Bowl • Dutch Oven with Cover • Sauce Pot with Cover
Large Sautée Pan with Cover • Large Soup Pot with Cover • Basting Brush
Wooden Spatula • Tongs • Slotted Spoon • Colander • Paper Towels • Kitchen Towels
Kitchen Shears • Baking Sheet • Corkscrew • Measuring Cups and Spoons
Grease Splatter Screen for Sautée Pan • A Bunch of Plastic Deli Containers

NICE TO HAVE

Pepper Grinder • Charcoal Grill • Charcoal • BBQ Tongs • Roasting Pan with Rack
Herb Ruler • Microplane Grater • Wire Whisk • Duck Press • Vegetable Peeler
Ladle • Seed Spoon • Stainless Steel Bowls of Various Sizes • Ladle • Rubber Spatula
Cutting Board with Drip Groove • Rolling Pin • Bread Knife • Kettle • Mesh Strainer
Kitchen Twine • Pie Plate • Hand-Held Mixer • Cupcake Pan • Cake Pan • Culinary Glue
Asian-Style Ceramic Spoons • Plastic Wrap • Wax Paper • Mink Napkins
Lobster Cradle • Airtight Containers for Flour and Sugar • Oyster Shucker

RATHER USEFUL

Meat Thermometer • Fat Separator • Food Processor • Immersion Blender
Flameproof Baking Dish • Non-Stick Skillet • Spice Grinder • Molasses Timer
Plastic Cutting Board • Apron • Poultry Shears • Pastry Blender • Ice Cream Maker
Aluminum Drip Pans • Ramekins • Turnip Pipe • Hand-Held Orange Juicer
Stand Mixer • Kitchen Torch • Microwave Oven • Meat Mallet
Box Grater • De-Salter • Electronic Kitchen Scale • Mandoline Slicer
Cut-Resistant Gloves • Cracker Crisper • Wok with Heat Disperser Ring
Steak Knives • Extras of Everything

PREPOSTEROUS

Wooden Spoons • Garlic Press • Cheese Knife • Blender • Turkey Baster • Pot Holders
Set of Nesting Glass Bowls • Foil Cutters • Pasta Forks • Any Pizza Equipment
Anything That Uses The Internet • Custom Cutting Board That Fits Over the Sink
Potato Masher • Too Many Knives

NOTE

If you don't want to buy a piece of equipment, see if you can borrow it from a friend or neighbor, or see if there's a kitchen tool lending library in your area.

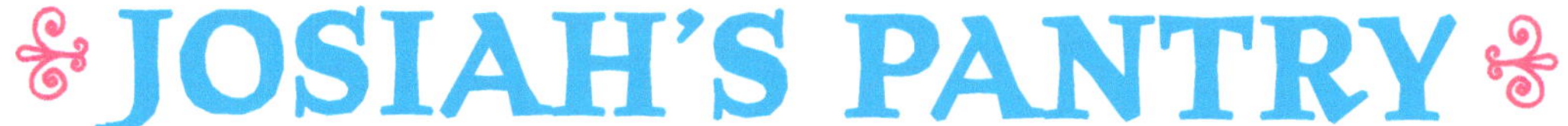

JOSIAH'S PANTRY

ESSENTIAL

High Quality Olive Oil • Imported Parmigiano-Reggiano Cheese
Onions • Carrots • Celery • Heads of Garlic • Red and Green Peppers
Cabbage • Lettuce • Avocado Oil or Other Salad Oil • Butter • Salt • Pepper
Local Honey • Cans of DOP San Marzano Tomatoes • Packages of Nice Pasta
Pinto Beans • Potatoes • Sugar • Flour • Dijon Mustard • Barbecue Sauce
Soy Sauce • Mexican Hot Sauce • Milk • Apple Cider Vinegar • Bread
Fresh Eggs • Whole Chicken • Boneless Skinless Chicken Breasts
Italian Sausages • Seasonal Fruits and Vegetables • Wine • Tomato Paste In A Tube

Fresh and Dried Herbs (basil, bay leaves, chives, oregano, parsley, rosemary, thyme)
Spices (chile powder, cinnamon, coriander seeds, cumin, cumin seeds, fennel seeds, garlic
powder, onion powder, paprika, red pepper flakes, yellow mustard seeds)

NICE TO HAVE

Fresh Olives • Pickles • Seasonal Mushrooms • Surprising Mustards • Various Cheeses
Beef & Chicken Stocks • Confectioner's Sugar • Brown Sugar • Baking Powder
Bergamot • Baking Chocolate • Vanilla Extract • Vanilla Beans • Almond Extract
Horse's Pudding • Rice Wine Vinegar • Scallions • Potato Chips • Italian Breadcrumbs
Mandrake Root • Ground Beef, Pork & Veal • Stew Beef • Chicken Scraps for Stock
DOCG Chianti • DOCG Orvieto Classico • AOC Côtes du Rhône • Provençal Rosé

RATHER USEFUL

Shallots • Lemons • Limes • Heavy Cream • Apricot Jam • Pancetta • Mushroom Ketchup
Sesame Seeds • Poppy Seeds • Walnuts • Pine Nuts • Pistachios • Cashews
Food Coloring • Cuppycake Decorations • Whimbrel Thighs • Vermont Noodles
Sesame Oil • Ergot of Rye • Powdered Syrup • Sauternes • Vin Santo • Prosecco

PREPOSTEROUS

Canola Oil • Frozen Dinners • Bottled Water • Yogurt • Cream Cheese
Olio Lampante • Smoothies • Herbed Butter • Sour Cream • Tomato Paste In A Can
Macro Brews • Vodka • Steak Sauce • "Wagyu" Beef • Fictitious Cuts of Steak

NOTE

This list is simply the opinion of Josiah Frosting, don't get mad.

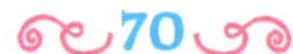

INTERESTING RESOURCES

THE FRENCH CHEF WITH JULIA CHILD
Featuring Julia Child. PBS, 1963-1973. Available on PBS.org.

IRON CHEF
Featuring Takeshi Kaga, Chen Kinichi, Hiroyuki Sakai, Masaharu Morimoto and others.
Fuji Television, 1993-1999. Available Online.

EMERIL LIVE
Featuring Emeril Lagasse. Food Network, 1997-2007. Available on FoodNetwork.com.

NO RESERVATIONS
Featuring Anthony Bourdain. Travel Channel, 2005-2012. Available on Travel Channel.

ITALY UNPACKED
Featuring Giorgio Locatelli and Andrew Graham-Dixon. BBC, 2013-2015. Available Online.

MY LIFE IN FRANCE
by Julia Child and Alex Prud'homme, 2004 Alfred A. Knopf

KITCHEN CONFIDENTIAL: Adventures In The Culinary Underbelly
by Anthony Bourdain, 2001 Harper Collins

DOWN AND OUT IN PARIS AND LONDON
by George Orwell, 1933

HOW TO GRILL
by Steven Raichlin, 2001 Workman Publishing

WATER, FLOUR, SALT, YEAST
by Ken Forkish, 2012 Ten Speed Press

THE PERFECT SCOOP
by David Lebovitz, 2007 Ten Speed Press

THE ART OF MEXICAN COOKING
by Diana Kennedy, 1989 Clarkson Potter

MASTERING THE ART OF JAPANESE HOME COOKING
by Masaharu Morimoto, 2016 Harper Collins

THE ACCOMPLISHT COOK –or– THE ART AND MYSTERY OF COOKERY
by Robert May, 1660/85, Reprinted 2018 Prospect Books

DR. FEGG'S NASTY BOOK OF KNOWLEDGE
by Terry Jones and Michael Palin, 1976 Berkeley Medallion Books

THANKS TO EVERYONE WHO HELPED FUND THIS BOOK!

Aaron White • Alicia Forrest • Allison Lake • Amy V Robertson • Ana
Arthur Butler • Carla Almeida & Family • Carolyn Warfield • Casa Valwardo
Charles Dooher • Chris Flynn • Christine Gourley • Danielle Morrison
Dava Guthmiller • David Laliberte • Deborah Levering • Delilah Faye Young
Elena Ariel Ivanov • Garrett and Helen • George A. Jones
Harry Merkin • Jenne Barbey • Johnny and Sue Johnson • Jules Benbow
Kathy, Millie and Chai - very good eaters! • Keith Gerstmann
Kevin Coughlin • Kim Hamilton • King G. Heiple Jr. • Koala Bear
kyrsten buzzard • Leona Chiarappa • Magnus & RoseZetta Lima
Marcya Rosecrans • Marissa Saidy • Mark Anderson • Mark Milloff
Marrio R. Lopez | @tikikaiju • Masanori Taguchi • Meg Gordon Sussman
Megan Sherret • Moog Kaltenbach • Morgan Uribe • Patrossamus!
Randy Morris • Reid Ritschard • Richard Knights • Sarah Freligh & Justin Ward
Sarah Hiatt • The Scullys • Sherine & Tom • Susan "Garden Arms" Stepanian
The Right Honourable Katherine Jane • Theun Kohlbeck
Trish Almeida • Voronwe Duende • Wizedog

...AND TWENTY OTHER RATHER GENEROUS PEOPLE!

SPECIAL THANKS TO

Allison, Suzi, Jen, Coral, Jon and Jason, who helped to make this book so much better.

MANY THANKS TO

MY BELOVED FRIENDS

Allison, Leopold, Pat & Kay, Jason & Suzi, Sherine & Tom, Susan & Trish, Jon & Marina, Ed & Valerie, Jen & Chris, Les & Tanda, Will & Danyelle

MY TEACHERS

Mark, Benigna, Bob, Karen, Helen, Ed, John, Jasmincka, Howard & Mark

MY FRIENDS & COLLEAGUES

Charles, Danielle, Eric, Kelly, Sean, Mike, Bert, Bill, Lane & Colin

THESE PORTLAND ESTABLISHMENTS

Division Wines, Stammtisch, La Moule, Dānwèi Cāntīng, Bollywood Theatre, The Star & Afuri

MY HEROES

Hieronymus, Albrecht, Marcel, Julia, George, David, Monty Python & The Sisters of Mercy

IN MEMORY OF

Raymond Larrett

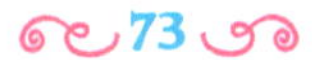

Publisher's Cataloging-in-Publication data

Names: Frosting, Josiah, author.
Title: The Frosting University kitchen workbook : an absurd but serious cookbook / written
and illustrated by Josiah Frosting.
Description: Includes bibliographical references. Portland, OR: Frosting University Press, 2020.
Identifiers: LCCN: 2020921285 ISBN: 978-1-7360245-0-8 (Hardcover) 978-1-7360245-1-5 (ebook)
Subjects: LCSH Cooking. Humor. BISAC COOKING / Comfort Food COOKING / Courses & Dishes /
General COOKING / Methods / General
Classification: LCC TX714 .F775 2020 DDC 641.5--dc23

Hardcover ISBN: 978-1-7360245-0-8
eBook ISBN: 978-1-7360245-1-5
Library of Congress Control Number: 2020921285

Printed On Demand by IngramSpark

Conceived, Founded, Illustrated, Written, Designed, Edited, Tested and Enjoyed by Josiah Frosting

Art Direction By Allison Lake
Additional Copy Editing By Susan Scully, Allison Lake, Jennifer Fenolio Faye & Jon Prugh
Additional Recipe Testing By Allison Lake, Jennifer Fenolio Faye, Coral Faye, Susan Scully & Jon Prugh

Based on an Exciting Original Idea by Josiah Frosting

Journal font designed by Zuzana Licko, Emigré Design
Harlean font designed by Laura Worthington, Laura Worthington Type

Don't be bland.

FU001 - 78 - 4141 - 165

First Edition